Simon Heffer was born in 1960. He read English at Corpus Christi College, Cambridge, and later received a PhD in history from that university. He has been deputy editor of the *Daily Telegraph* and of the *Spectator*, and a columnist for both. He now writes for the *Daily Mail* and is editor of *Mail Comment Online*. His books include biographies of Thomas Carlyle, Enoch Powell, Edward VII and Vaughan Williams, and the guide to English usage *Strictly English*. He is currently writing a book on Victorian England, to be published in 2013. He is married with two children and lives in Essex.

Simon Heffer

—

A SHORT HISTORY
OF POWER

nh Notting Hill Editions

Published in 2011
by Notting Hill Editions Ltd
Newcombe House, 45 Notting Hill Gate
London W11 3LQ

Designed by FLOK Design, Berlin, Germany
Typeset by CB editions, London

Printed and bound
by Memminger MedienCentrum, Memmingen, Germany

A CIP record for this book
is available from the British Library
ISBN 978-1-907-90320-5

www.nottinghilleditions.com

To Michael Burleigh

Amicus verus est avis rara

To rule means to exercise power, and power can only be exercised by one who possesses it. The direct connection between power and rule is the fundamental truth of all politics and the key to all of history.

Ludwig August von Rochau, *Gründsätze der Realpolitik: angwendet auf die staatlichen Zustände Deutschlands*, 1853

Contents

– Preface –

I wanted to use the format of an extended essay to discuss in a relatively short form a great subject that had arisen out of wide historical reading over the last thirty years: why has history taken the course it has? We live in an age of first-class historical writing, with book after book revealing new depths of scholarship and research. The use of documentary evidence in particular, and the opening up of archives that had hitherto been closed either because of repressive regimes that controlled them, or because of statutory time limitations, have put new detail and exactitude into the writing of history.

However, the motives behind the events that are now so accurately recounted are often either taken for granted or otherwise not rendered clearly. I concluded that there was one abiding reason, at least since Thucydides began to record history 2,500 years ago, why events had from time to time changed an apparently set course: and that was the pursuit of power. However, it was not as simple even as that. Power is, I argue in *A Short History of Power*, pursued by states for one of four reasons: the need to achieve territorial security; the determination to impose a religion on a society; the pursuit of wealth; and the desire to impose an ideology on a society.

In every conflict current in the world elements of these four themes can be detected. However, in different epochs in world history, one theme has tended to predominate over the others. We see how territorial questions were of prime consideration in the ancient world; how the period from the Crusades through to the Reformation and Counter-Reformation was dominated by the pursuit of power in order to assert control over the religious feelings of peoples; how from the time of Spain's and Portugal's global explorations from the late 15th century through to the British imperial heyday of the late 19th the pursuit of power was stimulated by the pursuit of wealth; and how, hard upon the influence of Marx and Nietzsche, the 20th century became a battleground of ideologies.

The essay's conclusion describes how each of these themes is active in current international relations, and how power remains the key to all history. As such, the book takes issue with the theme of Francis Fukuyama's celebrated 1989 essay *The End of History*, in which he argued that the end of the Cold War and the dissolution of the Soviet empire represented 'the end of history as such: that is, the endpoint of mankind's ideological evolution and the universalisation of Western liberal democracy as the final form of human government'. It argues that such optimistic theses as Fukuyama's are typical of ages of plenty; I contend that this essentially Whig interpretation of history had its origins with Macaulay in the age of expansion in mid-Victorian England, and that Fukuyama was similarly lulled into optimism by the relentless 'progress' of the West in the post-war period. Now, in an age of global economic contraction and an international terrorist threat, the situation looks less predictable, and the future less bright.

The book also looks at how history has seen a constant shift in international relations, with different great powers at different periods, and the apparent impossibility of maintaining great power for anything resembling permanency: Greece, Rome, its successor the Holy Roman Empire, Spain, Britain, America have all had their moments of glory: China, India and possibly Brazil appear to be waiting their turn. Now, it is economics rather than force of arms that dictates these shifts of power; but, as throughout history, economic strength has allowed the possibility of great armed forces, and the martial strength that helps protect the economic power of the state. But even states with great armies can, in a world more and more ruled by global market forces, go quickly into decline. A decade ago America seemed invulnerable. Now, its loss of confidence after the attacks of 11 September 2001, its misjudgements in foreign wars and foreign policy, and its decision to go on a borrowing spree have made it appear impoverished and vulnerable, and left the way open to more efficient and ruthless rivals to challenge its pre-eminence in the world. History tells us that such things have always been the case; and the current decline of America reminds us that history's themes continue to recur.

For this reason, I conclude that Western, democratic civilisation is on the defensive, and that the expected victory of liberal values is far from certain. History shows us that it is an error to imagine that the values of even the most successful and powerful state will not, at some point, be challenged by another polity with a different prevailing view; and that it is equally mistaken to imagine that states operating systems of repression are, or ever will be, things of the past. My conclusion confirms the tone of realism: 'The first step in the defence of democracy must be to recognise that the desire of others to assert their power, for their reasons, is as pervasive as our own. If we use our liberties to allow our own value system to be undermined, then we shall lose them.' I hope those who read my book will have a clearer idea of the motive forces of what we call history, and therefore of what history is.

One

– Introduction –

Why has history taken the course it has? Has it been an accident – down simply to fate, or time and chance, or the operation of some unseen and unseeable hand? Or have there been great, inevitable, themes of human behaviour that have recurred to change the way societies have developed throughout the millennia in which history has been recorded? And do they continue to influence events now, and defy projections that a different, more permanent world order is being instituted?

If we look at why events have happened we soon realise that the same handful of reasons recur. In his 1989 article *The End of History*, written as the Soviet empire evaporated, Francis Fukuyama wrote: 'What we may be witnessing is not just the end of the Cold War, or the passing of a particular period of postwar history, but the end of history as such: that is, the endpoint of mankind's ideological evolution and the universalisation of western liberal democracy as the final form of human government.'[1] His thesis cannot yet be proved. He was conscious that the final, universal acceptance of democracy would come slowly. Much of the two decades since he outlined his thesis has set it back. Liberal democratic values seem to be in retreat. Fukuyama's vision seems ever more Utopian, compromised by eternal forces.

The rise of Islamist extremism since al-Qaeda's formation in the late 1980s does not in itself prove him wrong; but the refusal by certain Islamic states to condemn al-Qaeda's activities; or to make any reforms themselves that might lead them towards democracy; and the hostility of a wider number to the American-led 'war' against Islamism, suggest a settled new world order is some way off. Nor are these the only impediments.

America's response to the threat it perceives against itself has also compromised its own liberal democratic values. Former Soviet satellites in Eastern Europe have espoused democracy, but Russia itself is a sham democracy – a tyranny in disguise – as are some former Soviet republics. Russia still interferes in democracies, such as the Baltic states, that it resents having had carved out of 'its' territory. China may be moving towards capitalism economically but it remains repressive socially and in terms of human rights, and makes no pretence of espousing liberal democracy. Much of the Middle East and Africa are despotisms of one stripe or another. Latin America has its beacons of democracy – notably Brazil – but elsewhere has repressive regimes and some states – including Mexico – on the edge of anarchy.

The desire for power, sovereignty, hegemony and control is basic, and will always ensure that tyranny exists. But force and repression are not now the only methods of pursuing power. Three of the world's most formidable polities – America, China and Russia – adopt economic means, with armed force to support them. America's recent excursions in Iraq and Afghanistan, Russia's assault on Georgia in 2008 and China's use of force against some of its own minorities have all exemplified this. Actions by these powers in the first decade of the 21st century show that history is not simply about progress: disputes will still be settled by force, just as in Thucydides' time. Those disputes may arise for reasons that are tenuous or disingenuous, just as when the Spartans and the Athenians fought each other.

In the mid-1990s Samuel P. Huntington's response to Fukuyama was that clashes between civilisations would replace those between ideologies.[2] As we have recently seen, those clashes may be armed. Democracies strive to avoid war because of the perceived immorality of bloodshed in the democratic model and to protect their standards of living. However, so long as there are nation states with distinct national identities, and so long as religion plays a role in the world, the four reasons for the pursuit of power by polities that I will detail in this essay – land, God, wealth and ideology or minds – will continue to cause turbulence, and will throw up ideas that challenge the settled order.

Carlyle's assertion that 'the History of the World

. . . was the Biography of Great Men' has echoed for the last 170 years.[3] Events have happened, and continue to happen, in sovereign polities because powerful individuals, whether as tyrants or despots operating by fiat, or acting in concert with others as oligarchs, or with a democratic mandate from an electorate, take certain decisions. What motivates those decisions? Has it not most usually been the urge to assert control, or to resist its assertion by others? The argument of this essay is that the desire to acquire, preserve and exercise power, and the autonomy that the possession of power brings, have been the driving forces behind the account of events in the past that is called 'history': and that they will continue to be the driving forces behind events in the future. Such things are inseparable from human nature. The history of the world is not the biography of great men, but the history of power.

The question of what in any polity constitutes the basis of power – the basis of the right to rule that political unit – has troubled philosophers as long as there have been polities. Aristotle observed that 'there is also a doubt as to what is to be the supreme power in the state: is it the multitude? Or the wealthy? Or the good? Or the best man? Or a tyrant?'[4] The choice now is simplified. It is between democracies and non-democracies.

The four basic motivations behind the pursuit of power have been, first, territorial, when a polity seeks to expand in order to extend its power, or to enable a better defence of itself; second, the pursuit of wealth in order to provide better standards of living and security; third, the determination by leaders and the elites that support them to impose their political doctrines and their associated values on others; and fourth, war made or conquest undertaken in order to spread or impose a religious orthodoxy.

These motivations have from time to time changed the course of history, a concept Gibbon described as 'little more than the register of the crimes, follies and misfortunes of mankind'.[5] Such a dismissal is typical of his cynicism; yet it is surprising that that cynicism did not lead him to a wider denunciation of history, which is that it has so often been (and so often continues to be) propaganda. This was especially true of English historians writing in the two or three generations after him, in the age of Carlyle, Macaulay, Green and Froude. Nor was it the case – as a glance at those four names should confirm – that it was just the Whigs, or progressives, who engaged in propaganda: the Tories, in seeking to shore up their own vested interests, were just as capable of it. Historians have propagandised to paint an edifying picture of their heroes: by playing down the importance of the lust for power to the course of history.

Gibbon himself was a propagandist, highlighting the negative effects of Christianity and venting his own hostility towards organised religion. Carlyle, in advancing the great man theory of history, praised Cromwell and Frederick the Great; and in denigrating democracy praised both of them again. In *Past and Present* he presented the counterpoint of feudalism in the middle ages; an era he had already, in his essay *Chartism*, celebrated as 'the most perfect feudal time'.[6] Froude's history of Tudor England promoted his belief in Protestantism and his hatred of Catholicism, notably in his treatment of Queen Mary. Macaulay depicted the aftermath of the Glorious Revolution as having had such an enlightened outcome that the rightfulness of the revolution could not be questioned. Green's *History of England* sought to define a specific national story and national identity at a time when Britain had established itself as the world's leading power, and needed a clear back-story. Motley's building-up of the Dutch republic reflected in part his belief in the excellence of the American republic from which he came. Historians have always had an agenda, reaching back to Herodotus with his occasionally apophthegmatic style advancing morsels of wisdom, or Thucydides shaping the political history of Greece. One cynic who understood this too well was Goebbels. He read Carlyle's *Frederick the Great*, with its narrative of Prussian success against sometimes fearsome odds, to Hitler in the bunker as the Russians pulverised Berlin.

In 1931, in *The Whig Interpretation of History*, Herbert Butterfield exploded the myth that history was a comfortable story of progress, telling a tale of advancement towards a goal of perfection. 'In reality,' he wrote, 'the historian postulates that the world is in some sense always the same world and that even men most dissimilar are never absolutely unlike.'[7] He ridiculed the division of humanity by the whigs into 'men who furthered progress and men who tried to hinder it'.[8] Most important, he exposed the fallacy of imposing on to the people and events of the past the values and ideas of the present, which only distorted the perception of those people and events. The world is always the same world; and the driving forces of history are constant, even if at some epochs one theme will assert itself more strongly than others.

To argue that the pursuit, acquisition, retention, defence and loss of power are the fundamental causes of change in history confronts head-on this Whiggish notion of history. All major 'historical' events have been motivated either by the preservation of the degree of privilege that comes with sovereignty in all its forms (including the spiritual), or the desire to secure or expand it. The pursuit of power throughout history has largely been a manifestation of the aggressive and competitive nature of men (and almost always men): that is clear from Thucydides onwards.

War has been the obvious and frequent manifestation of the pursuit of power. The occurrence in the 20th century of two world wars, and the growth in the early 21st of international terrorism conducted by primitive means of warfare, show that this most basic means of the pursuit of power is still with us. Wars have ended empires, changed boundaries, precipitated revolutions, altered demographies and devastated economies. They have also stimulated (and at times been stimulated by) technological advances and social change. The Great War precipitated a range of upheavals from the Marxist revolution in Russia and the coming of Hitler to the emancipation of women in Britain.[9] The Second World War was mother of the nuclear weapon, the Cold War and the end of the British empire. At most times in history the means of pursuing power has been predominantly martial; at others it has been a mix of force and diplomacy, with the latter replacing the former progressively in Western civilisation since 1945. Power may also be sought through economic strength, the possession of territory and natural resources, religious influence or the extension of one ideology at the expense of another. However, these qualities have often been acquired or asserted as the result of the use of force, and as such may from time to time provoke those at whose expense they have been acquired to regain them by force.

In his work *Power and the Pursuit of Peace*, the

Cambridge Professor of International Relations Sir Harry Hinsley said there were two kinds of forces that brought about war: he called them 'impersonal and man made'. He said the first were the conditions that were 'given'; the second were the 'man-made contribution'.[10] Marx, also quoted by Hinsley, suggested that wars were the consequence of the existence of independent states: in other words, the prevalence of national interest (however that is defined) will cause polities to fight each other from time to time. Since Hinsley (and Marx) wrote, certain aspects of international relations have changed.

Hinsley's ideas of the causes of war cry out for greater definition. States may be faced with 'given' conditions – the presence of a wanton aggressor, for example, such as Poland and Czechoslovakia were faced with from Nazi Germany in 1938–9; or they may manufacture them. The pursuit of influence caused Napoleon III to take the bait offered him by Bismarck and to provoke the Franco-Prussian war. This from the Prussian point of view was an opportunity for them to conduct a classic war of territorial expansion, and to assert themselves as Europe's main continental power, though that was not what Napoleon III thought at the time; he would have categorised it as a war of 'honour'. But wars, like the tango, require two participants; and Bismarck wanted the war to display Prussian might against another European power, in the interests of securing the unification of Germany under Prussian leadership that was necessary to seal Germany's place as the principal continental power. The Romans had followed a similar course almost two millennia earlier. Most other European wars since the treaty of Westphalia in 1648 were either designed by one power or group of powers to stop the spread of territorial influence of another (such as the wars of the Spanish succession) or were opportunist acts of aggression to expand control by a state over neighbouring polities (such as the Napoleonic wars), and to seek to make challenges to the aggressor state more difficult.

Richard Ned Lebow, a professor at Dartmouth, has placed great emphasis on the role of honour in causing wars: typically, a power is slighted by another and determines to exact satisfaction, much in the fashion of a duel between Prussian noblemen. He cites as his authority the sociologist Max Weber, saying that 'international politics for Weber is driven by the desire of states to have their superior worth recognised'.[11] Many wars can be explained away thus, in pursuit of Weber's idea of 'power-prestige'; but there are equally persuasive alternative explanations of the motives behind conflicts. While it is considered gratifying for a nation to be more powerful than other nations, we have to ask: why? Usually, the answer is that it is good to be secure, good to be wealthy, and only as a secondary consideration is it good to have people doing as the centre of power directs them: not least because security and wealth are threatened if they do not.

Much of what follows is drawn from Europe and the world as subsequently colonised and developed by old European powers. I have sought to avoid what Edward Said dismissed as 'Orientalism', the distortion of the history of the East by writers from former imperial powers who seek to justify their culture's hand in dominating, for a time, another that they have deemed inferior. Said wrote, defining his term, that 'my contention is that Orientalism is fundamentally a political doctrine willed over the Orient because the Orient was weaker than the West, which elided the Orient's difference with its weakness'.[12] However the Europeans, by the 16th century, had shown that they were simply better equipped than the Muslim world in particular at expanding their reach and therefore their power: they were better sailors and navigators, and therefore became more adept at creating the wealth that helped shore up expanded polities.[13]

Africa discovered its own economic power first through the slave trade, then through the development of natural resources. The export of Western culture, whether Christianity or Coca Cola, has often put those people who feel they are being culturally colonised on to the offensive, with responses in recent times as varied as those of Osama bin Laden or Vladimir Putin. Now, in an age when environmental considerations have become paramount, power may be equated with possession of resources as much as with having money or an armoury: having oil, gas, or land that can be cultivated to provide not just food but biofuels may hold the key to a nation's power for the future.

Often, the collective force of organised politics in a polity has been the engine of the pursuit of power; sometimes, though, it has relied on one individual of resolve, will or determination to lead and motivate others in a common project. Outside the scope of my argument is consideration of how individuals become leaders, which belongs to a work of psychology. It may be worth just touching on the most famous cases here. Some like Alexander the Great, Peter the Great and Frederick the Great were born to their sobriquets: others acquired greatness, often by ruthlessness and brutality. In the last century Hitler, Stalin and to an extent Mao were inadequates who learned how to manipulate and to impose systematic terror.

Leaders may inspire through moral example, and when they do it lends weight to the 'great man' theory of history; or they may inspire through fear, which normally requires a state apparatus to carry through the threat behind the fear. For no one man can be an army: for any autocrat, despot or dictator to make an impact on history he has required not just mass support, but the support of a ruling elite. This applies as much to the morally uplifting as it does to the gangster. Leaders from Julius Caesar to Kaiser Wilhelm II, and a rash of more contemporary figures, have all experienced the collapse that comes when an elite withdraws its consent. The most powerful dictators have been those who can command the widespread loyalty and secure the connivance of others. Those dictators may themselves have had the will to pursue power, which has been crucial, but they have in the end acted as the agents of a polity. Dictators in the 20th century, like emperors two millennia earlier, had to act with a measure of consent from an elite that gave them political support and guaranteed the raising, financing and engagement of armed forces. The motivations of individuals and castes have been unquestionably significant in shaping history; but one man has never yet won a war.

Aristotle saw tyranny as a perversion of royalty and oligarchy as a perversion of aristocracy: but he saw democracy as a perversion of constitutional government. 'In a constitutional government the fighting-men have the supreme power, and those who possess arms are the citizens.'[14] Clearly, the way in which some of the terms Aristotle used are defined has evolved in the last 2,300 years. 'Democracy,' he wrote, as if to clarify the point, is 'when the indigent, and not the men of property, are the rulers'. Ever since the Persian empire challenged the Greeks in the sixth century BC historians have recounted how the battle for power has influenced events. One can see from their accounts that because of the drive for power and the instinct for sovereignty between nations and polities there must always be conflict of one sort or another between them, or the ever-present potential for it. Both Aristotle, with his assertion that man is a political animal, and Plato, with his contention that those with the good fortune to step outside the cave and see sunlight rather than just shadows on the cave wall should seek to shape the destinies of those stuck inside, are relevant to this argument.[15]

The motive forces have changed from time to time, with one theme or another dominating epochs in history. The world has over the last two or three millennia experienced periods of territorial expansion, empire-building for the purposes of the pursuit of profit, attempts to enforce religious doctrines and attempts to impose political systems. In the last century the world has experienced all four of these: Hitler sought territorial expansion (and the infliction of a fascist ideology on his own people and on the territories he conquered); Stalin sought to impose an ideology in satrapies in Eastern Europe and sought territorial expansion, or at least the establishment of client states, in order to do it; militant Islam today claims to be seeking to restore the Caliphate and mount jihad against infidels; and now the Chinese, in their investment in impoverished African states, seek to find new sources of profit in their experiment with capitalism and as part of an apparent strategy to supplant America as the world's foremost economic power.

The exercise of power has throughout history had both domestic and international dimensions. The emphasis of my argument will be on the latter, not least because for most of history power (whether territorial, economic, religious or ideological) has often been acquired by one polity at the expense of another, and has therefore had a strong bearing on what is now called international relations. In this context we can also see a clear difference between a world in which there was no balance of power – such as under the Roman empire – and one that does have, or seeks to have, one. The pursuit of a balance of power, which was in great part the story of Europe from the Dark Ages onwards (though only wittingly since the late 17th century), is a key part of the narrative of the history of power: and the rise of America from the Great War onwards has given a new dimension to that narrative, just as the rise of new economic powers such as China, India, Brazil and possibly Russia threatens to alter it again.

In his last state of the union address, on 6 January 1945, Roosevelt said that 'We cannot deny that power is a factor in world politics, any more than we can deny its existence as a factor in national politics.' This had always been true; and because of the central importance of power to politics, so the pursuit of power has dictated the course of history, which has ever been at the mercy of politics. It is now time to consider in detail the four principal motivations for that pursuit.

Two

– Land –

'In a pre-industrial age, power was equated with the possession of land and the population it carried, or with a trading monopoly in tropical produce with its glittering promise of a surplus of bullion.'[1] In explaining how this leads to conflict with other aspirant nations, the Oxford historian John Darwin added, in his history of empire, that 'dynastic ambition and mutual suspicion raised the territorial stakes. In Western Europe, the four-cornered struggles of France, Spain, Britain and the Netherlands over the previous century [the 18th] had turned on the question of whether Britain or France would be the dominant power in Atlantic Europe, with effective control over the maritime access to Europe's Atlantic extensions in North and South America.' Darwin reminds us that one of the key influences upon events has been the building of nations. City states turned into principalities, which themselves merged into countries. A common tongue, ethnicity and culture were often the driving force, but nothing accelerated the process more than realising the existence of a common enemy.

Greater size meant greater status and greater security: though it also brought with it greater risk of attack from jealous powers who wished to guard their own position of dominance, or to establish one. Acquiring contiguous territory helped secure a polity's own borders and see off potential aggressors outside them. More land brought with it the means of wealth, additional population to increase the size of armed forces and to create more scope for patronage. It also helped put greater geographical distance between the core of a state (such as its seat of government) and territory controlled by potential aggressors, making it harder for aggressors to complete an invasion.

Nations are both a physical-political construct and an ideological one. The concept of the balance of power, where strong nations (originally within Europe) could co-exist without war, grew out of this. In the age of imperialism, notably in the 19th century, the location of tensions between the European powers shifted temporarily to other parts of the world, notably Africa; but direct conflict in the Great War brought them back to continental Europe. The balance of power could not survive the determination by one nation to become the predominant power in the world, and to attempt to do so by an exhibition of force.

The compulsion to use territory as the basis of power has been constant since antiquity. In 510 BC the Athenians expelled their tyrant, Hippias, after a seventeen-year rule of exceptional cruelty. Hippias then devoted his life to plotting a means of returning; and this included, in 499 BC, his seeking the help of the Persians. He went to Sardis, capital of the Persian colony of Ionia, and sought to persuade the satrap there, Artaphernes, to conquer Athens. Artaphernes was a ruler of considerable sway, being the brother of King Darius I of Persia. In retaliation for this the Athenians decided to help the Ionians to rebel against Darius, who had conquered many Greek territories in the previous twenty years or so. The Athenians, who had hitherto had no quarrel with the Persians, sent envoys to Sardis to ask them to mind their own business.

Artaphernes, unused to being addressed in such terms, retorted that if they sought safety they would best acquire it by restoring Hippias. However, at that moment the Ionian Greeks asked the Athenians to help liberate them from subjection to the Persians. Despotism thus sided against democracy, suggesting the struggles for power of more than 2,000 years later. The first victory was to democracy, since the Athenian forces temporarily occupied and burned Sardis, until driven out by superior Persian forces. King Darius was nonetheless outraged at the insult contained in the attack on one of his possessions. He therefore set out to assert his power in the traditional fashion: first, by laying waste to Ionia, demonstrating that he would control the destiny of that territory; and then by the conquest of Greece.

Darius sent envoys to Greek cities demanding they submit to him. Many did, having heard of the punishment inflicted upon Ionia. Athens and Sparta alone did not, so Darius determined to compel them by force of arms.[2]

Persia was the first great classical empire. As Creasey put it, it had by the time of the Battle of Marathon in 490 BC 'shattered and enslaved nearly all the kingdoms and principalities of the then known world', and had done that in the space of just fifty years.[3] Although territorial conquest had brought the Persians wealth, that was a secondary consideration to the security it had brought to its despotism. The desire to add Greece to the portfolio was but the latest step in this acquisitiveness, and for the same reason: that if the territory of the existing empire was threatened, then the threat had to be removed. Darius does at least appear to have been sincere in this belief: some of history's more recent such expansions, such as Hitler's into Czechoslovakia and Poland, were about acquiring territory to populate with Germans.[4] The acquisition of territory compounds the problem for those resisting the imperialist. At least, by 1939, what Creasey called the 'known world' had expanded, and there were nations and polities around the globe who could, and did, send men to confront Hitler. Had the Athenians not stood and fought at Marathon only the Spartans would have stood in the way of a Persian conquest of all Europe. Rome had not yet established its own power, and the rest of the continent was peopled with barbarians of one description or another. Such was the potential disposition of Darius's power that the entire course of European, and therefore quite possibly world, history might have been changed had Athens rolled over.

Because of the importance of territory war has always been an inevitable means of securing or acquiring it, often with unforeseen consequences to the course of history. Violence has always been a fundamental human instinct and since primitive times has held an important place in shaping the natural order of civilisation. Once city states and nation states defined by the limits of their territory came into being it was inevitable that force would be employed to protect and expand them. Augustine of Hippo defined a just war as one that was defensive or designed to recover possessions: 'In order to possess the combination of moral and physical courage necessary to defend their property and rights against foreign invasion, civilised nations must feel convinced that they have the power of securing that property and those rights against all domestic injustice and arbitrary oppression on the part of the sovereign.'[5]

The default condition of some early polities was to be warlike: the Romans are a notable example. As Finlay points out, the Romans were helped vis-à-vis Greece in being a single city state, with unified objectives of expansion: the Greeks they sought to conquer were a collection of city states with diverse objectives. Worse for them, 'the Greeks regarded war as a means of obtaining some definite object, in accordance with the established balance of power. A state of peace was, in their view, the natural state of mankind. The Romans regarded war as their permanent occupation: their national and individual ambition was exclusively directed to conquest. The subjection of their enemies, or a perpetual struggle for supremacy, was the only alternative that was presented to their minds.'[6] The existence of other, potentially rival and certainly wealthy polities was reason enough for the Romans, in this frame of mind, to attack and seek to subdue them: no further provocation was needed. That peoples such as the Greeks preferred to concentrate not on martial matters but on the development of their civic virtues provided a rich opportunity for the implementation of such a philosophy. As Hitler looked at the Czechoslovaks in 1938, and even at the British, he adopted a similar attitude.

One of the more important examples of this was the challenge to Rome posed by Jesus Christ, and the decision by Pontius Pilate to calm down civil disorder in Judaea by having Christ executed on a charge of treason against Rome – the claim that he was 'King of the Jews' – that even Pilate himself might not have considered was actually treasonable (depending upon what account one believes in the gospels, and how one translates them). Christianity then posed such a challenge to Rome that the state sanctioned persecution of members of the cult for almost 300 years.[7] In the end, the spread of Christianity was so formidable that Rome was forced to allow it as a religion within the empire by the Edict of Milan of 313 AD.

Although the desire to subjugate neighbouring territories in ancient empires was justified as a means of securing threats to those empires' borders, inevitably other consequences flowed from territorial expansion. Wealth, whether in the form of tribute or taxation, or in the acquisition of a workforce or natural resources, was the most obvious. If the conquered land could identify a common enemy with the conqueror, the conqueror also acquired more military power. These considerations set a standard for subsequent ages. Many of the Roman colonisations during the Republic in the fifth to first centuries BC may have been undertaken for reasons of security, but they greatly enriched Rome. Though they set out to acquire territory, the Danes, Angles and Saxons who undertook expropriatory raids and attempts at colonisation in England in the Dark Ages were pursuing wealth. There were no security issues, any more than there were on the part of the Vikings who headed further across the north Atlantic. It has been argued (by the American historian of international relations Richard Ned Lebow, among others) that reasons of honour inspired William of Normandy to invade England in 1066, but this dresses up an opportunistic desire to increase Normandy's wealth by allowing the Duke to become King of England and acquire its land and resources.

The inevitability of conflict between societies that wish to protect or acquire territory sometimes causes history to seem little more than an account of attempted or successful conquests. These may take into account the 'great man' theory of history, already discussed; but the territorial consideration has other consequences. These include expansion, subjugation, the imposition of will and culture, the creation of empire and the promotion of certain sorts of civilisation: far from being designed, these have often been the results of time, chance, sudden necessity and opportunism. The acquisition of territory often has not settled matters, but instead become a new source of conflict. The establishment of perhaps the largest empire the world has ever seen – the Mongol empire of Genghis Khan in the 13th century, which is estimated at one point to have covered 22 per cent of the world's land mass – is a fine example of this. Genghis unified the nomadic Mongol tribes and undertook ruthless conquest of neighbours who, earlier, had sought to subjugate the Mongols. As with the origins of the Roman empire, the Mongol empire expanded after territory was acquired to reduce the security threat. It spread from the Sea of Japan to eastern Europe, occupying not merely modern Mongolia, but much of China, Russia and central Asia too.

Kublai Khan, Genghis's grandson, sought to move the capital of his vast empire to Beijing. This aggrieved the Mongols, and began the process of splitting up the empire, and its decline. The sheer impossibility of ruling so great a mass of territory without provoking divisions was reminiscent of what happened in the Roman empire in the fourth and fifth centuries. By the 14th century Mongolia was weakened by rebellions, and the Chinese developed their own policies of provoking conflicts between factions among the now-marginalised Mongols, re-sulting in the contraction of the empire.

Territorial expansion brings with it powers of patronage that shore up the adventurers and chal-lengers for power who succeed in such enterprises. This creates the basis for a structured state, formal-ising power within a political structure and making it harder to overthrow, and imposing other cultural forces and values that help modify a subjugated so-ciety to the model of the conqueror's. The Roman republic and empire were formed in this way; so too the first German Reich; and on a smaller scale, the unification of England by the Duke of Normandy as Conqueror. A common culture across smaller Euro-pean states during the modern period, the legacy of earlier but subsequently dissolved hegemony, also provided a drive to unification and nation-building. Spain and France achieved this between the 15th and 17th centuries; in the 19th, both Italian and German unification were indicative of that cultural-historical force. Bismarck had settled after the Austro-Prussian War of 1866 that his state would lead that unification and not Austria; but Hitler's justification for the *Anschluss* in 1938 was a historic union of the German-speaking peoples such as had last been seen in the Holy Roman Empire.

Territorial expansion has also helped improve the defence of a polity, as was seen during the Peloponnesian Wars of the sixth century BC and the establishment of the second German Reich and the Hapsburg empire. On a much smaller scale, England's security as part of the island of Britain was settled first by the incorporation of Wales into the Kingdom, then by the Union with Scotland in 1707 – though the latter had Jacobite aftershocks in 1715 and 1745 that had to be seen off first.

The glory that comes from conquest is not merely an end in itself: it also helps perpetuate the momentum of a polity's development and demoralises less successful rivals. Territory is a means of enhancing the status of a polity, adding to its strength in terms of providing wealth and armies, and supplying the means of patronage. It gives a polity status in the world and causes it to have greater influence over the course of events than would otherwise be the case. History too often suggests that expansion also reflects the basic human instinct of the urge to control, a trait common to the regimes of William the Conqueror, Napoleon, Hitler and Stalin. It also illustrates the desire, strong right until early modern times, for the establishment of dynasties: something not unknown in modern democratic politics, as both the Kennedy and Bush families show. Territorial empires in pre-modern times needed to be secured by military or naval power; in modern times by that or by consent. When both were lost, empire as a form of power was lost. Spanish imperial ambitions finally died at Trafalgar with the defeat of its navy, whereas British imperial power was confirmed by the victory of hers. Hitler's empire failed when his forces were overrun; but the Soviet empire died when its subject people withdrew their consent, and the last Soviet emperor understood the political and strategic impossibility of seeking to enforce Soviet will by force of arms. The manifest defeat of an idea is now seen to be just as catastrophic for the maintenance of territorial power as the defeat of an army or navy.

Rome's might was built after first securing the peninsula of what is now Italy. Its foreign policy was directed to this end exclusively in the first instance. This meant securing Cisalpine Gaul and dealing with Carthage and Macedonia. Roman statesmanship had it that Rome could only be strong – and therefore secure – if its rivals were weak, and this meant capturing or laying waste their territory. Carthage lost Sicily and Sardinia, then lost sovereignty, then was obliterated. The Roman policy of clientage, to stop rival powers from being strong, required more and more conquest. A determination to be surrounded by weak states soon led to them becoming provinces. Theodor Mommsen, whose work on Roman history left him with the reputation of the greatest classicist of the 19th century, argued that once overstretch was achieved and the Parthian kingdom formed it ended in Islamification because a new power centre had opened up in Asia.[8]

As I have mentioned, the argument that wars begin because of matters of honour or status, and that significant changes in the course of history occur as a result, has been applied to the invasion of England by William of Normandy in 1066. William was an ambitious duke who, by obtaining the throne of England, would be a king. Yet he would have that elevation in status because of one important consideration: the acquisition of territory. Without territory he would have no position. The Normans had always understood this. Having originally been Vikings, they consolidated their position in Normandy by annexing more territory to the west before they crossed the channel. In their understanding the basis of power was land and the wealth and manpower that came with it. William's aspiration was legitimate as he was a cousin of Edward the Confessor, the childless king who died in 1066, and his claim to the throne more dynastically legitimate than Harold Godwinson's, who became king by election.[9]

The conquest created a new rivalry in Europe. William was, as King of England, the peer of the Capetian King of France: but as Duke of Normandy he was his vassal. The history of almost the next 400 years, to the end of the Hundred Years War, shows how dynastic wars are essentially about territory: for there is no point being a king without a realm over which to exercise power and from which to exact finance or tribute. Once the Angevins or Plantagenets, by a mixture of war and marriage, had by the mid-12th century wrested control of more than half of France, the nominal kings of France had little choice, if their own position were not to be questioned, but to try to wrest it back. Attempts to do this by force in the 1150s were unsuccessful and the second half of the century saw the summit of Plantagenet power. The accession of King John in England in 1199 provoked an offensive against his lands in France by Philip II, who by the end of 1206 had secured everything apart from Gascony. King John, his territory reduced to just England, Ireland and one province of France, found his throne insecure because he was undermined by the loss of territory. Aquitaine supported Queen Eleanor, and

Anjou, Maine and Touraine Arthur of Brittany, leaving John vulnerable.[10]

A century later dispute over the succession in the Capetian dynasty in France seemed to the English aristocracy to provide an opportunity to regain 'their' lands, forfeit for a hundred years because of John's military weakness. Isabella, daughter of Philip IV of France, was wife of the King of England, Edward II: their son, who would be Edward III of England, was thus also in the line of succession to the French throne. By 1328 all Philip IV's three sons had succeeded as king and had died. Salic Law had been applied to prevent a female successor. The English had also fought an unsuccessful campaign in Gascony and had lost everything but Bordeaux and a strip around it. This crisis of succession and sting of defeat seemed to supply both reasons of honour and dynasty to provoke a new conflict: but what really lay at its heart was the desire by the English to regain their land, and fear by the French that they would do so. Edward III considered himself, under the standard English interpretation of feudal law, the rightful king of France after the death of his last surviving uncle: the French would not have it. Using Salic Law as an excuse – Edward's claim being through his mother – they put Philip VI on the throne instead. Philip used the pretext of the overthrow by the English of David, King of Scotland, to drive the English out of what was left of their

Gascon lands in 1337: and so began the Hundred Years War. By the end of it England had just Calais left; and the idea of France and England as nations, bringing with it a firm understanding of the ideology of territorial possession and the identification of a people within demarcated lands, had been properly settled.[11]

The Thirty Years War, though seen as a product of the Reformation, was partly motivated by territorial considerations. It was expected in Europe that the expiration of the Twelve Years Truce in 1621 would cause the Spanish to try to re-conquer the Netherlands, something they could do only if allowed to take their armies through the Electoral Palatinate in the Rhineland. It was with this in mind, rather than simply a desire to re-assert the authority of the Catholic church in the Netherlands, that led to Spain's sending an army to assist the Emperor in 1621. Similarly, the Danish intervention in the war after 1625 was not simply because of a religious fear of the spread of Catholicism following the successes of the Emperor and his allies (the Palatinate was under Catholic control by this point) but a fear of loss of sovereignty over Danish territory. France's intervention in 1635 (when it declared war on Spain) and 1636 (when it declared war on the Emperor) had no religious motivation at all. Richelieu wanted to engage in a fight against the Habsburgs because their territories were too close to France's for comfort. His support of the advancing, Protestant Swedes from the north through Pomerania can be seen as an early but authentic attempt at securing a balance of power, using Sweden as a check on the power of France's neighbours. When this developed into a war with the Spanish the final victory of the French brought about the beginning of the decline of Spain's international power, and set up France as the predominant European power until the defeat of Napoleon. The Treaty of Westphalia that ended the war in 1648 also set the pattern of self-governing territories within the Holy Roman Empire.[12]

The War of the Spanish Succession was another early indication of the importance of the balance of power, and how that balance was influenced by territorial possessions; the rest of Europe feared a union between the French and Spanish thrones under the Bourbons that would have eclipsed other European powers. This idea, though, was also ideological: not in terms of a system of thought, but in the principle of other nation states being allowed to grow too large. The French would also have acquired Spain's massive overseas empire and the wealth that went with it. By the early 18th century, the possession of territory and the resources it could bring had become the principal factor influencing events; but the notion of the importance of territory and sovereignty over it would become a key component of the ideology of nationalism over the following 250 years. This was not, however, new. An ideology such as this had arisen out of the Hundred Years War, which ended up making two nation states with territorial integrity: England and France.

Frederick the Great said in 1743 that 'of all the states from the smallest to the biggest one can safely say that the fundamental rule . . . is the principle of extending their territories'.[13] All powers in the history of the world that have been legitimately regarded as great have held sway over significant territories; and their decline has been marked by the loss of them. Within a century of Frederick's having written those words there was one conspicuous example of his doctrine being applied: the expansion of the newly independent United States of America to fill the land mass between Canada and Mexico. Much of this new territory was acquired by either diplomatic or commercial means rather than conquest, such as the Louisiana purchase and the acquisition of Florida from Spain at a time when Spain's grip on its American empire was failing. However, war was necessary on two occasions against the British former colonial masters; when America sought Oregon and other parts of the north-west in 1846 Britain solved the question by diplomacy and not force. There were also the Indian wars against American natives who regarded much of the newly acquired land as theirs, and a successful war against Mexico to secure California and settle a boundary dispute about Texas. The expansion, especially when conducted by force, helped forge the concept of American nationalism.

In the old world, the Ottoman power of the early modern period declined as the Austro-Hungarian empire encroached upon its lands in one direction, and the Greeks and Slavs from others. The defeat of the Ottomans outside Vienna in 1683 was crucial for the power of Austria-Hungary and the beginning of the two-century process of driving Turkey out of Europe. Spain, a formidable power in the 16th century, having been damaged in the Thirty Years War and having lost its territories in South America, was of little consequence by the 19th. Frederick's Prussia became an empire with the unification of Germany and then sought to emulate other European powers by finding colonies on other continents. Power became as much about reach – the ability to send a navy or army to far-flung parts of the earth – as it did about holding land itself. Britain dwindled as a power when its empire was dismantled; the Soviet Union was a power in a way that Russia was not under the Romanovs, and would not be again under Putin, because it did not and now does not control Eastern Europe or the former Soviet republics. Considerations of the motives behind most non-continental imperial expansion by European powers, outside the territorial integrity of the motherland, belong to the chapters on Wealth and Minds.

When Frederick was seeking to consolidate and further expand his power after the Seven Years War, and developing the machine of the Prussian state, a still primitive Russia under Catherine the Great was noting the vacuum opened up by the decline of the Ottoman empire. She embarked upon successful wars against the Turks, finally fulfilling Peter the Great's ambition to take territory from them in the Ukraine, Crimea and elsewhere around the Black Sea. She did this not least with Prussian support – which Frederick came to regret because of the added strength the acquisitions of Ottoman territory gave to Russia. Then the two powers connived in the partition of Poland, which allowed Frederick to link up Prussian lands and have a largely unified, modern state. From the 18th century onwards, though, nations started more carefully to weigh up the benefits of expansion against its risks: defending wider frontiers in continental empires, or the overstretch entailed in defending imperial territories far from home, even across the seas, which caused such problems for George III over his American colonies. The dynastic wars in the early 18th century are about territorial expansion for security and commercial reasons, before the idea of the balance of power finally matured. Reasons of state then trump reasons of dynasty in pursuing territorial wars.[14]

This can be seen abundantly in the policies of France immediately post-revolution. France's attempt under Napoleon to found a colony in Egypt in the late 1790s was motivated by the desire to show herself to be an expansionist imperial power like Britain. France believed this would be possible because of the vacuum being created by the failing Ottoman empire, something Russia was also seeking to exploit. Later, Napoleon wanted to lure the Russians into war after his defeat of Prussia in 1806 with the aims of defeating them heavily and keeping them out of European politics for the indefinite future. Russia was equally motivated to be a European player, which was one of the reasons why it ultimately beat Napoleon. It was not merely successfully defensive: it was motivated by the desire for expansion of influence to be successfully aggressive. The Treaties of Tilsit in 1807 temporarily satisfied the desires of these two expansionist powers for land and wealth at the expense of Prussia. They settled common imperial borders in central Europe, providing the security needed for the pursuit of prosperity, enlisting Russian support for France's war against Britain and French support for Russia's designs on the Ottoman lands. However, the annexation of Galicia to the Duchy of Warsaw, under French auspices, was one of a series of provocations that caused Russia to start planning an offensive war in Poland to protect its interests; and Napoleon pre-empted this by seeking to secure more eastern territory for France, and to defeat Russia to improve his own empire's security.

However, he became unable to supply his army once it had taken Moscow, and it was reduced to a shell during the retreat through Russia and Lithuania by starvation, disease and desertion. This turning point in Napoleon's fortunes – for it proved to the subjugated powers of central Europe that he and France were after all not invincible – demonstrated the dangers of overstretch from territorial expansion, and its unintended consequences.[15]

The Congress of Vienna of 1814 directed expansionism to outside Europe. It was preceded by the Treaty of Chaumont, which specified the four great allied powers and the way European affairs would now be conducted: diplomatic power would seek to supersede martial. The century from Waterloo to the Great War is sometimes depicted as one of peace and progress thanks to the rise of diplomacy; this conveniently forgets how the political context that brought about the war in 1914 was caused by wars and other acts of territorial aggression, especially during the last third of that century, that went contrary to the principles of Vienna.

Chief among these were the policies of Bismarck that brought about German unification in a contiguous territory. Hinsley says that Bismarck's wars were conducted 'for reasons of state, not on nationalist grounds'.[16] Yet the reason of state was to form a nation, and in Bismarck's case the nation was a territorial concept rather than a metaphysical idea.

Nationalism was a territorial concept that would mutate into an ideologically racial one for a later generation of Germans: however, in the 1860s those in Prussia who wished to push forward the idea of nation did so by seeking to control the territory of others. The Franco-Prussian war of 1870–71 has been seen as France's responding to a slight against it by Prussia. In fact, there was no slight. The French ambassador to Prussia had buttonholed King Wilhelm I on his morning walk in the spa of Bad Ems and asked him to guarantee that no Hohenzollern candidate would be presented for the vacant Spanish throne. The King politely declined to give such an undertaking. Bismarck, alerted to this matter in a dispatch from a courtier, obtained the King's permission to publish the dispatch. However, he edited it first to make it appear that the King had insulted the ambassador, and vice versa. He expected this would provoke France to declare war, and it did. This was nothing really to do with honour: it was to do with Bismarck's determination to make Prussia a world power, which Napoleon III was too obtuse to perceive. Honour and standing are in fact points covered by the importance of territory, and also have an ideological underpinning: the idea that what a nation has, it holds, and in medieval Europe onwards, the idea of national identity and the importance of the framework of nationalism, which is itself ideological. There is no doubt that Richard

Ned Lebow is right when he argues that the desire for esteem and recognition are important; but those desires are fulfilled by more fundamental and less metaphysical means, such as by the acquisition of territory and the wealth and influence that goes with it.[17] And, once acquired, territory may have to be defended by force.

Nationalism, as I have mentioned before, is an ideological concept. When it comes to nation-building it is hard to discern a boundary between aggression undertaken for territorial or security reasons, or that for ideological reasons. Once Germany became the main continental power it had to decide whether it wished to use its territory to secure itself, or as a base from which to aggress and dominate the rest of Europe. If Kaiser Wilhelm I was in two minds about this, and content (as he saw it) simply to teach his neighbours a lesson of respect towards the Second Reich, Hitler, when his turn came, was in no doubt that territory, and the labour force, resources and wealth it brought with it, were prime considerations in German policy.[18] Kaiser Wilhelm II had stumbled when he had his chance to make Germany not merely a European, but a world power. Hitler was not going to be so cautious.

Territorial considerations did not merely influence the course of European history, or of Europe's overseas empires. In 1894 the Sino-Japanese war was caused by Japan's fear of territorial insecurity because of Korea. This fear may have been fed by the application of a European perspective to it. A Prussian adviser to the Japanese, Major Klemens Meckel, called Korea 'a dagger pointed at the heart of Japan'. There were not, however, merely security considerations. Korea's mineral deposits would be invaluable for industrial Japan. A little later, and on the other side of the globe, the Spanish-American War of 1898 was also a conflict of mixed causes: of America's getting an empire and expanding the Monroe doctrine of territorial security. In the Americas as in Europe, where physical annexing was not taking place, the metaphysical equivalent – the establishment of spheres of influence – was happening instead, so that regional powers could maintain their strength and, in an age where conflict was supposedly to be resolved by diplomacy, their credibility.

The Great War ended, for a time, the notion that diplomacy could trump arms. The causes of the war are complex. That it started because Gavrilo Princip shot Archduke Franz Ferdinand and his wife in Sarajevo in June 1914, and Austria's honour then had to be satisfied, is a simplistic description of the reasons. The roots of the war can be traced back to the Treaty of Berlin of 1878, which had sought to resolve territorial conflicts in the Balkans following the Russo-Turkish war. The Congress recognised the independence of Serbia, Montenegro and Romania, but aimed to keep Constantinople in Ottoman hands rather than have the city ceded to Russia. However, among other details it allowed Austria-Hungary to occupy Bosnia-Herzegovina, and ordered that Russia's Black Sea fleet be prevented from passing through the Straits of Constantinople in time of war. Austria-Hungary was concerned about the pan-Slavic movement and the threat of rebellion by Slavs against imperial rule; the destabilising effect this would have had on Germany alarmed Bismarck, who convened the Congress. The main European powers were also keen to arrest Russian territorial expansion into the Ottoman empire to the Mediterranean, into what was a British and, to a lesser extent, French sphere of influence.

The newly sovereign Serbia was angered by the decision, endorsed by Russia, to allow Austria-Hungary to occupy Bosnia-Herzegovina. This combustible situation was aggravated 30 years later when Austria-Hungary decided to annex Bosnia-Herzegovina, a move that gave Princip his excuse in 1914. The annexation took place on 6 October, the day after Bulgaria had declared independence from the Ottoman empire. Austria-Hungary also coveted the Sanjak of Novibazar, land between Serbia and Montenegro that would be necessary for a physical union of the two states. Serbia was already militant in its opposition to Austro-Hungarian hegemony, and the annexation provoked Serbia further. There had, however, been traffic between the foreign ministers of Austria-Hungary and Russia about opening up the Straits of Constantinople as a quid pro quo for the annexation: the accounts of the talks from the two sides do not exactly resemble each other. The Russians felt cheated by the Austrians; the Austrians released diplomatic documents from the preceding 30 years that showed Russian complicity in what had happened in Bosnia. Russia was humiliated; Serbia, angry at the annexation, was neutered. Russia's relations with Austria were especially poisoned. All the pieces were in place from October 1908 for the Great War, and the issue was territorial. All that was required was the ultimate provocation, provided by Princip.[19]

Nature abhors a vacuum: when the Russians were defeated by the Japanese in 1905 the great beneficiary was Germany, now unchallenged on the continental landmass, and with France weakened because of the blow to its ally. The events in the Balkans in 1908 were greatly to Germany's advantage, which was not least why that power rejected the idea of a formal conference to try to settle the matter. The idea of *Weltpolitik* was already well established, not least as a means of building up a rivalry to the British empire, even if this meant acquiring territory in Africa and the Pacific. First and foremost, Germany had to be the unquestioned European power; and from 1912 wanted a war in order to establish itself as a world power.[20] After the Archduke's assassination, a failure by Austria-Hungary to make an example of Serbia might have encouraged Romania to seek to annex Hungarian territory that was populated by ethnic Romanians. In this resolution Austria-Hungary had the full support of the opportunist Germans.

The disregard conquerors often displayed for their subject peoples, their culture and their institutions inevitably inspired opposition. When overstretch or the rise of decadence occurred, and governance became weak, it allowed a resurgence in national identity, which would serve as the basis for those peoples to rise up and seek to challenge the conquest they had undergone. As Finlay argues, this seemed to happen in Greece.[21] When governance and the systems of governance remained strong, those systems tended to hold, sometimes for centuries: Finlay contends that 'the international system of policy by which Alexander connected Greece with Western Asia and Egypt was only effaced by the religion of Mahomet and the conquests of the Arabs' – in other words, they lasted more than 700 years.[22] Alexander had commercial intentions leading on from his conquests as well as strategic and security ones. The pursuit of his prosperity was not furthered by grinding down his conquered peoples, but by what Finlay calls 'the principle [of] the amalgamation of his subjects into one people by permanent institutions'.[23] He tore up the rulebook that says conquerors 'augment their power by the subjection of one race to another'. Despite the fact that the Greeks wanted his rule to end and to assert once more their own liberty, he designed a system of governance for them that benefited them. Therefore, the Greeks had progressively less incentive to waste blood and treasure seeking to overthrow the new system. (Something similar happened in England after 1066, when over a period of two or three centuries the incoming Norman population slowly integrated with that of the incumbent Anglo-Saxons, imposing institutions and, to an extent, culture, but finally adopting (with modifications) the language of the conquered and sharing a new prosperity with them that grew through the Middle Ages.)[24]

In the fourth century AD Constantine I's decision to move in the later part of his reign to Byzantium effectively began the separation of the Eastern and Western Roman empires, but also arrested the tendency of provinces in the East to go their separate ways. The problem with trying to control a wide expanse of territory, whether then or in the 19th and 20th centuries, has always been one of overstretch. Between the death of Arcadius in 408 and the accession of Justinian in 527 'the absolute power of the emperor was now controlled by the danger of foreign invasions, and by the power of the church'.[25] Finlay implies that this signals the emergence of an early variant of constitutional monarchy:

'the interest of the sovereign became thus identified with the sympathies of the majority of his subjects'.

Justinian shored up the Eastern empire by exacting revenge – and in the process securing his territory – against those tribes who had sought to dismember Roman authority. He set about 'exterminating the Goths and Vandals, and . . . arresting the progress of the Avars and Turks'.[26] At his succession Justinian had bought peace with the Persians, who were a constant threat to his eastern borders, by paying over 11,000 lbs of gold to the Emperor Chosroes. Instead of using peace to consolidate his power at home, Justinian preferred to take the opportunity to settle scores with Goths and Vandals on his southern perimeter in Africa, Sicily and Italy. Finlay asserts that Chosroes' 'jealousy' at the economic and strategic power these new conquests brought Justinian prompted him to renew the war.[27] He invaded Syria in 540, crushing Antioch (which had refused to pay him a ransom of 1,000 lbs in gold) and extracting ransoms from several other Syrian cities that learned from Antioch's mistake. The war lasted for twenty years, leaving borders at the end more or less unchanged from those before it began, but requiring Justinian to pay an annual tribute of 30,000 pieces of gold to Chosroes, for whom wealth had become the main measure of his status and power relative to other rulers. He also taught Justinian the lesson that Roman territorial power was secure only so long as it had the money to ward off challengers to it.

Some theorists, such as Lebow, argue that fear is a motivation to start wars. Yet fear is a response, and it requires analysis of what it is a response to. It is usually because another power aggresses or threatens to aggress because the polity that is in fear has something the aggressor wants. When powers have claimed fear as a reason to start war – as Hitler did when mendaciously claiming Poland was aggressing against the Reich in 1939 – it is normally an act of the most intense cynicism. Fear is normally a response to a threat to take territory; or to impose a new system of values, religious or ideological, upon a people within that territory not hitherto subject to it. Huntington touches upon this point in describing the nature of communal wars, which he says 'may occur between ethnic, religious, racial or linguistic groups'.[28] What these four categories have in common is a cultural flashpoint. All except the religious have usually had territorial associations: an assault on an ethnic or racial group, whether or not also defined by its religion or language, often happens because another power seeks to secure territory in order to shore up its own position in power. Serbia's conduct in the former Yugoslavia in the early 1990s was a recent example of this. Most notably, the conflict in the Middle East between Israel and the proponents of a Palestinian state invokes all four of Huntington's categories, but is fundamentally about territory and sovereignty. Where religion is not an issue in such wars the dispute may have ideological origins, as I discuss in the chapter on Minds. Often, though – as Huntington also argues – the sheer proximity of two deeply opposed cultures can be enough to promote conflict between them, especially if fears are whipped up by those who seek war for purposes of territorial acquisition, or to further their religion or an ideology, and if there are sharp changes in demography.

Naked pursuit of territory is often dressed up with some other excuse, and Hitler was far from being the first to do it. Charlemagne was ruthlessly territorial, yet sought to justify the creation of the First Reich by expanding the boundaries of Christendom. Even in the late eighth and early ninth centuries land grabs were viewed as provocative, but wrapping them up in the mantle of Christianity added some legitimacy to what was an extremely temporal and materialistic exercise. Lebow talks about 'appetite' as provoking conflict, and again he is right. Yet appetite, which in this context is a metaphysical concept, will usually have tangible stimulants. Lebow suggests that appetite was what drove William the Conqueror to invade England in 1066. Yet William and his nobles in Normandy had grown up in a culture of ambition, and that meant territorial expansion. What he understood to have been Edward the

Confessor's promise to him of the English throne was, when it failed to be honoured, a perfect excuse for him to seize the land by force, and take his duchy to the height of its power as a Kingdom. Having defeated Harold at Hastings, and having over the next few years secured his kingdom, William had acquired land, wealth and with them influence in Europe.[29] As in the Franco-Prussian conflict 800 years later, a rival had presented him with an excuse to establish an expanded power of his own. As has been noted, most territorial expansion, whether by conquest in battle or annexation by other means, also expands the influence of the polity responsible by adding to its physical and manpower strength. This has been as true in modern times as in ancient ones – as the growth of America from thirteen colonies to fifty states, or the massive growth in Soviet power after 1945, both showed. That one still exists but another does not exemplifies the need to maintain not just the means, but also the will, to defend sovereignty over territory when it is challenged.

Empires also require wealth and security to survive, and the existence of these will affect the level of will. The Spanish empire in the Americas crumbled after the humiliation of Spain by Napoleon when forced to give up Louisiana (which then covered a tract of America from the Gulf of Mexico to Canada), which sent a signal to independence movements across the continent that the imperial master was vulnerable and lacked both the will and the force to retain its possessions.[30] The British empire was undone by the impoverishment of the mother country after the Second World War as much as by any anti-imperialist ideology on the part of the Attlee government: and it was financial considerations and the evidence of overstretch that caused the Conservative administration of Harold Macmillan to lose the will to hold on to the remainder of the colonies in the late 1950s and early 1960s. But empires also end because of hubris: the second German Reich was one example, but not so clear a one as the third. The miscalculation of Hitler in entering into a martial struggle with nations whose forces would in the end outnumber his, and whose economic and productive capabilities (secured by military superiority, notably in the air) were less exhaustible than his, was fatal.

In our time, and so far as the advanced, democratic powers are concerned, the experience of the two world wars of the 20th century has essentially put an end to warfare between Western nations as the means to undertake an exchange or shift of power. Rivalries are now pursued by other means, whether diplomatic or economic; while, ultimately, power and the means to command or alter the course of history now reside with those who have the most destructive arsenals, something no longer dependent upon the possession of extensive territory but sometimes coincidental with it.

The activities of Hitler and Stalin in the last century do, however, prove that the ancient and primitive desire for territorial expansion as the fundamental means of establishing and securing power did not die with the medieval period, or with the acquisition of the European colonial empires. The ideological drive behind these expansions is described later in the chapter on Minds. If one has been tempted to see history as about progress, and about a growing sophistication in the aims of those people and polities whose actions shape it, that view should be tempered by the understanding that its most basic, almost feral, motivation has remained strong right down to the present day. Hitler's war was about land: the fulfilment of his explicit desire, expressed in *Mein Kampf*, for *Lebensraum*. 'The foreign policy of the folkish state must safeguard the existence on this planet of the race embodied in the state, by creating a healthy, viable natural relation between the nation's population and growth on the one hand and the quality and quantity of its soil on the other hand.'[31] He continues: 'Only an adequately large space on this earth assures a nation of freedom of existence. Moreover, the necessary size of the territory to be settled cannot be judged exclusively on the basis of present requirements.' He adds that Germany was only pretending to be a world power in 1914 because of an inadequate relation between population and territory. War broke out in 1914 as the culmination of a series of squabbles about territory, imperial and otherwise. The implosion of the Ottoman empire allowed Russia to move in to the Black Sea, ensuring its hegemony and access to warm water. Hitler, for his part, took land wherever he could, never expecting to have anyone else fight him over it.

Until September 1939, he was right. As far as other European powers were concerned, the pursuit of territory at the expense of other sovereign democracies belonged to another era. They attempted to keep this territorial aggressor at bay by means of diplomacy: but Hitler had contempt for diplomacy, and for the rules that Metternich had attempted to set for international relations. Once more, territorial considerations would prevail; and despite Hitler's defeat, the thirst for control of territory as a means of building and consolidating power has continued to the present day.

Three

– God –

M any of the wars that have redistributed power and influenced the course of history have
had an ostensibly religious motivation. Until recently this was regarded as a pre-modern phenomenon:
but a new relevance has been given to this motivation by the rise of Islamist extremism since the turn
of the century. There is a mixed message in the Bible
about war. The Old Testament sanctions it, provided it is conducted on behalf of God and aimed at
fulfilling His purposes.[1] This most obviously echoes
Islam, but also the Judaic tradition, in which wars
are fought for faith and not for any temporal considerations. The New Testament regards it as hor-
rific, and has a message of peace: 'And he shall judge
among the nations, and shall rebuke many people:
and they shall beat their swords into ploughshares,
and their spears into pruninghooks: nation shall not
lift up sword against nation, neither shall they learn
war any more.'[2] Those who shaped the Protestant
settlement in England after the Reformation had no
doubt about the compatibility between Christianity
and war. The 37th of the 39 Articles of Religion in
the Book of Common Prayer, 'Of the Civil Magis-
trates', includes the pronouncement: 'It is lawful for

Christian men, at the commandment of the Magistrate, to wear weapons, and serve in the wars.'

The Roman empire, which had begun as an operation to protect its civilisation by annexing the territory of those who threatened it, saw one element in that protection as being the persecution of Christians. By the fourth century it had become their protector. The initial hostility to it was caused by the refusal of Christians in the empire to engage in Caesar-worship, which the Romans took as evidence of subversion and treachery. In the past, the Romans had tolerated religions and religious cults so long as they did not present a threat to the established order or seek to undermine it. Constantine's own conversion to Christianity in the fourth century supposedly came as a result of his having had a revelation of Christian symbols in a dream on the night before the battle of the Milvian Bridge in October 312. He imputed his subsequent victory over his rival Maxentius to the protection of the Christian God. By the end of the century Christianity had become the state religion of the Roman empire, with predictably harsh punishments for those who chose not to observe the religion in the way the authorities demanded. As under paganism, a sense of orthodoxy was essential to the rulers' *amour propre*.

In an age when organised religion was of profound importance – which one might date from the ninth to the 19th centuries in Christendom, but from the middle of the seventh century and constantly thereafter in the Muslim world – and faith was still all-pervasive, unquestioned and deep, the desire by a polity or polities to impose a specific religious doctrine on a particular land, territory or people was a prominent factor in causing conflict and influencing the course of events. Often this imposition came as a result of conquest for other reasons, such as with the spread of Catholicism through Latin America after the arrival of the Spanish, or even of Anglicanism wherever the English or, later, British flags were planted. However cynical many rulers were, especially by the time of the Renaissance, some still felt it a genuine matter of conscience not just that their own faith should be enforced within their realms, but that they had a duty to promulgate it elsewhere too. The Emperor Charles V, in his resistance to Islam to the east of his territories, his determination not to let the Protestant Reformation adhere in the Netherlands, and his support of the Inquisition in the Americas, embodied this trait better than most.[3]

Historians cite both St Augustine of Hippo and St Thomas Aquinas as proponents of the just war theory. In his book on the Crusades Jonathan Riley-Smith writes that Pope Gregory VII found 'in Anselm of Lucca a partisan who, through a careful reading of the Fathers, above all St Augustine of Hippo, would build a convincing case for Christian violence as something which could be commanded by God, was at the disposal of the Church and would, when properly used, be an expression of Christian love.'[4] Augustine, in *The City of God*, had stressed that war was justifiable in defence of the weak and innocent, and not as an aggressive measure. He wrote that 'it is the wrongdoing of the opposing party which compels the wise man to wage just wars', and further justified his argument by saying that 'For even when we wage a just war, our adversaries must be sinning; and every victory, even though gained by wicked men, is a result of the first judgment of God, who humbles the vanquished either for the sake of removing or of punishing their sins.'[5] Thomas Aquinas developed this by adding that wars such as Augustine had defined as just needed to be waged by a legitimate authority, such as the state, and needed to have the establishment of peace as their aim rather than gain or punishment.

The fathers of the Church took, however, little account of cynicism, or the scope their theories gave to the less scrupulous in finding reasons to wage war. Religion would be a useful cover for baser motives in starting conflicts. Whether on occasion religion really was the cause of any given war, or simply cited as its cause, it would from Roman times to the present day lead to profound changes in the course of history. There is no doubt, however, that any attempt to promote heresy caused deep concern among Christian rulers because of their fears about what it would do to men's souls and their hopes of the eternal life. Equally, among cynical rulers both in secular life and in the church, heresy was a threat to their authority, wealth and power.

Such absolutist views were not confined to Christianity. The Prophet Mohammed enjoined his followers to pursue jihad. One interpretation of that command was to take the faith of Islam into lands of the infidel. The result was a change in the course of history even more profound than that resulting from Constantine's support of the Christians in the fourth-century Roman empire. In the seventh century Islam expanded first with victories against the Byzantine empire and the Sassanid empire of the Persians. This conquest of the Middle East was made easier by the shortages of money and manpower in the two defeated empires because of their own years of warfare against each other. However, the unity of purpose brought to the Muslim armies by the common faith of their soldiers and commanders also contributed to the speed of their success. [6]

Islam further expanded early in the eighth century with the victory over the Visigoths in Spain: indeed, had the Franks not defeated them at the Battle of Tours (or Poitiers) in 732 they might have had France too, and indeed the rest of Europe. Charles Martel, the victorious leader of the Franks, might have considered his enterprise that of saving the Frankish empire, which then covered much of what is now France and western Germany. His victory certainly secured the Carolingian empire for the next century, paving the way for the rule of Charlemagne. In this sense his motivation in the fight was purely territorial, and with a view to securing the secular power that comes with territory. However, generations of historians have described Tours as one the most decisive battles in the history of the world, in terms of its effects on the course of history, and have categorised Charles's achievement as having saved Christianity.[7] The resultant Holy Roman Empire gave spiritual power a political dimension, and lasted for 1,000 years – from Charlemagne's coronation in 800 to Napoleon's winding-up of the entity in 1806. The wealth and authority of the Christian Church in pre-Reformation Europe made it a polity in itself, and in time it attracted opposition just as other secular polities did.

Although the Muslim army Charles took on was an army of invasion, with a determination to secure territory in France as it had in Spain, the empire it sought to create was not driven by secular considerations of the sort normally satisfied by the acquisition of territory. It was about spreading the word of the Prophet, though doing so in a way that seemed to go beyond religion. Jihad, or struggle, was aimed at conversion or subjugation: the boundaries have always been blurred between Islam as a religious force and as a political or ideological one. Centuries later, when Saladin was extending his power, he came to see that doing so depended on the ability to extend patronage, which fundamentally required territory. Even the pursuit of a religious faith, as in Saladin's battles against the Crusaders, required a secular underpinning to provide the material means to do it. As Tyerman puts it, 'each conquest had to be followed by another'.[8]

From the 11th century onwards the Seljuk Turks of central Asia sought to expand their territory into the Byzantine empire; and the force of their passion for Islam was matched by the decline of the Christian empire they were attacking. Defeat led to factionalism within Byzantium and this lack of unity allowed further incursions by Turks. Byzantium's fortunes ebbed and flowed, periods of recovery in them being thanks to assistance from the presence of Crusader armies in the Byzantine empire from the end of the 11th century. When these armies from Christendom sought to regain Christianity's holy place in Jerusalem, the language employed to justify the expedition was initially purely religious: Jerusalem was to be liberated to 'drive out the heathen'[9] and to free the churches there from 'abominable slavery'.[10] However, once the Crusade had been successful, the opening up of trade possibilities made the Holy Land additionally attractive, not least to the devout Christians of the mercantile ports of the Italian peninsula. The Levant had been a prime market for traders in the Roman empire, and this possibility was now restored. However, from 1180 onwards Byzantium fell into chaos, with factionalism and weak leadership leading to a failure to secure its borders. Turkic armies attacked again, but the final proof of Byzantine incompetence was when Constantinople was sacked by soldiers on the Fourth Crusade in 1204. In the battle of faiths there seemed no question that the followers of Islam had the greater inspiration: and in the long term this would prove decisive.

The faltering of Byzantium led to the creation of the so-called Latin empire, which sought to establish itself as the proper successor to the Roman empire, and it held Constantinople until 1261. The aristocratic descendants of the ousted Byzantines, who had formed the Nicean empire, then managed to overthrow a Latin empire impoverished and reduced by war against both Bulgarians and Greeks. On regaining Constantinople they restored the Byzantine empire. However, the Turks took this period of instability as an opportunity to resume their own incursions into Christian lands; and over nearly the next two centuries there were to be conflicts between Islamic and Christian armies over the territory. Two civil wars in Byzantium during the 14th century allowed the Turks to take almost all the Byzantine empire; and by the end of that century the Byzantine emperor held his throne only as a vassal of the Ottoman sultan. That this rivalry had a religious core was shown by the dispute in the 1390s between Sultan Bayezid and Manuel II, the latter having been condemned to death by the former. Manuel was reprieved on the condition he built a mosque in Constantinople, and allowed a Turkish colony there: he refused, and instead summoned help from Europe in the form of a new Crusade. This only delayed the inevitable. When Constantinople finally fell to the Turks in 1453 it was because no other Christian nation had the resources to intervene and stop it.

Political opportunism was a regularly occurring element in the desire of rulers and nobles to extend Christianity. Constantine's own support for the faith can be seen as a means of supplying himself with the means to establish a power base in the east, and creating a new and more secure seat of governance. As has been noted, the establishment of the Carolingian empire and the First Reich stemmed from a successful defence of Christianity but had far more than a simple religious purpose. The original call by Urban II in 1095 to liberate Jerusalem was prompted by a plea from the Byzantine Emperor for reinforcements to help drive the Turk from his lands to shore up his secular power. Crusading in the Baltic States became increasingly about the extension of German authority.[11] The Teutonic knights were the first agents of this: and their activities were the reason why Prussia, and then Germany, extended as far east as Konigsberg. In 1226 Konrad, Duke of Masovia in what is now northern Poland, asked the Teutonic knights to help him defend his territory against pagan Prussians. Although the temporal notion of territory was once more at issue, the motivation behind the knights' assault on the Prussians was that they could be Christianised. The conflict on the fringes of Europe between Christendom and Islam, and the threat it was perceived to present to traditional European systems of power, lasted beyond the fall of Constantinople, right down to the Congress of Berlin in 1878, and the capital that Gladstone was able to make out of the Bulgarian atrocities against Christians. Today, there is a determination by Islamic extremists to challenge Western or Judaeo-Christian culture and to continue their prophet's campaign for the conversion of unbelievers to the Moslem faith. However, this also has a political aim – the restoration of the Caliphate – that further gives substance to the claim that the programme of al-Qaeda is more ideological than religious.

If paganism was the threat to what Christians defined as civilisation in northern Europe in the middle ages, in the south of the continent the threat was from Islam. Finlay says that Mohammed, by 'application of the aspirations of mankind after unity' had forged Arabia into one state under one religion.[12] In the seventh century Islam spread easily through those parts of the Roman empire where there was hostility to the established order. Where the indigenous people stood and fought, the progress of Islam was arrested, notably by the Greeks in Asia Minor. Charles Martel, a century later, found the same law applied at the Battle of Tours. Finlay speaks of Mohammed exercising a 'mighty influence . . . on the political, moral and religious condition' of those countries in the Persian and Roman empires that had been unwilling to accept the existing order.[13] He adds that 'a better religion than the paganism of the Arabs was felt to be necessary in Arabia; and, at the same time, even the people of Persia, Syria, and Egypt, required something more satisfactory to their religious feelings than the disputed doctrines which the Magi, Jews, and Christians indicated as the most important features of their respective religions.'[14]

Arabia was at this stage 'in the full tide of rapid improvement, eagerly in search of knowledge and power', and Mohammed seized the opportunity to exert over them what Finlay called 'his superior talents, and his clearer perception of justice and, we may say, truth'. He continues: 'His creed, "there is but one God", was a truth that insured universal assent; the addition, "and Mahomet is the prophet of God", was a simple fact, which, if doubted, admitted of an appeal to the sword, an argument that, even to the minds of the Christian world, was long considered as an appeal to God.' After 633 Caliph Aboubekr of Arabia, 'chief of the true believers . . . commenced those wars for the propagation of

Mohammedanism which destroyed the Persian empire of the Sassanides, and extinguished the power of Rome in the East.'[15]

When harnessed to individual polities, religion was also often an essential means of imposing the cultural values of the conqueror on the newly subject people: this applies as much to the growth of Islam after the seventh century as to versions of Christianity. It was also why there was such an energetic response to Pope Urban II's call for a Crusade to regain Jerusalem from the Muslims in 1095; and, to a lesser degree, why there were four subsequent Crusades to the Holy Land over the next two centuries, and why Christians sought to reclaim much of the Iberian peninsula from Islamic control, and to Christianise eastern Europe. The job was done until Philip III's brutal expulsion of the Moriscos from Spain to North Africa in 1609. This group were descendants of Muslims who had converted to Christianity in the early 16th century to be allowed to stay in Spain. As with Hitler's persecution of the Jews over 300 years later, this expulsion was more to do with perceived economic power held by that minority, and the belief that they were seeking to reproduce at a rate that would overwhelm the indigenous population, rather than the advertised conviction that they were insincere in their Christianity. Although the church locally sanctioned the expulsion on the grounds of the heresy of the Moriscos, Philip III also appropriated all their assets to the Spanish crown. A mark of the economic importance of the group was that Valencia, which had had a high concentration of them, went into a long economic decline.[16]

Religion, once enforced in a certain way, becomes a means of social control. This was also the motive of the Albigensian Crusade from 1209, aimed at stamping out heresy within Christendom, and why the Reformation – itself a desire, instigated by Martin Luther, to effect the transfer of religious power from corrupt prelates to genuinely Godfearing individuals in an early essay in democracy – caused such conflict. The salvation of men's souls remained important, and the concerns therein remained genuine, but the assault on established power and privilege that such heresies represented was a significant factor in the Church's resistance to them. As Christianity developed, so conflicts happened within Christendom, and not merely because of a united Christendom challenging, or being challenged by, other faiths. The Reformation was the prime example of this; and its consequences went far beyond the simply theological. As I shall argue later, the Thirty Years War only began as a doctrinal religious dispute, but soon was used by opportunists to develop power by territorial and financial means. However, even before that, the Reformation had given at least one worldly monarch the excuse he needed to attempt to undertake some imperial expansion. Philip II of Spain, who had in the 1550s been King of England, notionally launched the Armada to restore England to the Catholic faith: but just as important to him was adding it to his empire, which was then near the height of its greatness.

Equally, the time came when secular power became determined, for reasons of control, to assert itself over its sacred rival: as in the English Reformation and, in more modern times, the French law on laicity of 1905. The breaking of the power of the Catholic church had immense consequences for secular power throughout Europe (see the chapters on Wealth and Minds). It also contributed significantly to the establishment of the modern American state, whether through the initial emigration there of Puritans in the 17th century, or the mass emigrations of the late 19th/early 20th centuries. These were largely caused by the legacy of internal conflict left by the Reformation in many European societies, and by the depressingly traditional pastime of the persecution of Jews in Russia and Eastern Europe.

The advance of secularism has often brought with it deliberate assaults on the power of the church: Stalin, a former seminarian, promoted atheism in the Soviet Union, as did communist satellites such as Albania. When the Orthodox church could be useful to him – as in the hour of the Soviet Union's greatest crisis when under attack from the Nazis after 1941 – even Stalin moderated his view of it, enlisting its assistance to sustain his own and the state's power. China created itself as a republic in 1949 as a specifically atheist state, though that stance softened over the succeeding sixty years – provided religions conducted themselves in accordance with the outlook of the ruling elite. While not outlawing the Christian churches, Hitler sought to control them and acted ruthlessly against those who used the platform the church gave them to oppose Nazism. The church had often been explicitly associated with the previous ruling order – which, when monarchical, often claimed to rule by divine right – and so naturally became a target for revolutionaries. After 1945 the drive for freedom from repressive ideologies often had a religious focus, notably in the Catholic church in Poland, but also the revival of the Orthodox religion in Russia and the attempt to expand the Christian church in China. Paradoxically, the authoritarian and socially deeply conservative rule of Franco in Spain was closely associated with the Catholic church.

Throughout history, and in the writing of it over centuries, there has been an inclination to see the spread of religion as a desire to extend faith and, with it, the properties of civilisation and culture: the Victorians, such as Froude and Buckle, wholeheartedly believed this theory and were especially adept at spreading it. Gibbon, however cynically, was alert to its shallowness more than 200 years ago when he wrote the *Decline and Fall*. His assertions that organised Christianity led to the collapse of Rome seem specious, but the military and economic failures that caused the empire to fall were not helped by the diversions of Christianity.[17] In the last pages of his epic history he describes what happened to Rome as 'the triumph of barbarism and religion'.[18] It was clear from the use of religion within nations and then within their colonies that the enforcement of religious practices became a popular and effective method of social control and of the imposition of a culture and its values. Even the Crusades, however, soon turned into money-making exercises. The struggles around Europe after the Reformation were about protecting the established power structure, or even extending the reach of secular powers. When, after the Enlightenment, Christian states adduced religion as an excuse for expansion or aggression – such as Russia's assertion in the late 19th century that it had a claim to Constantinople because it was the imperial heir of Orthodoxy – it was as a fig leaf for more secular considerations. There is no such thing as a purely holy war, and certainly not that proposed in modern times by militant Islam. When the propagation of religion is seen instead as a strategy first to impose the political authority of a church, and second as an adjunct to the extension of secular power, the conventional perspective on the history of religion – and therefore of all history – changes.

The case can be made – and has been elo-
quently by Peter H. Wilson in his magnum opus
on the subject – that the Thirty Years War was as
much a war of political conflict, about the ideology
of sovereignty and the exercise of power, as it was
about religion.[19] However, it had its strongest roots
in the desire for Protestants to secure their rights
within the Holy Roman Empire and to ensure that
the Peace of Augsburg of 1555, which guaranteed
the religious rights of Lutherans in the empire, was
honoured: but because of the secular and territorial
power wielded by the Catholic church this also became a conflict about Lutherans retaining political
autonomy within the empire. Protestants also mili-
tated against the regime in France, through the wars
of religion of the late 16th century, until the Edict of
Nantes of 1598 granted toleration.

The immediate cause of the outbreak of conflict
in 1618 was the prospect of the succession of Ferdinand of Austria to the throne of Bohemia; Ferdinand
was a devout Catholic who wished to impose his faith
on his future kingdom, which was Protestant. But,
as mentioned in the chapter on Land, there was also
an aspect of European instability at that time that
was part religious, part territorial and part ideological: the prospect that at the expiration of the Twelve
Years Truce in 1621 the Spanish would seek to re-
conquer the Dutch Republic. This would re-impose
Catholicism on that state, but would also remove

its political autonomy. The re-conquest could only, though, be carried out with the co-operation of the territories under the sway of the Spanish Habsburgs' cousins in the empire, through which an army would need to pass to accomplish it. Another territorial aspect of the conflict was demonstrated in the tension between two Catholic dynasties, the Bourbons and the Habsburgs. Indeed, in that respect the power of the Catholic church was trammelled by the war, and in the end ceded authority in the matter to secular powers, notably the Bourbons.

The Enlightenment changed attitudes to religion, notably in seeking to remove its coercive aspects. Buckle traced the intellectual movement as having started with Bacon and Descartes in the 17th century, but the fuse burned slowly.[20] Temporal heads of state no longer felt themselves to be the agents of a religious orthodoxy. Voltaire praised Catherine the Great's leniency towards Protestants and Catholics ('we ought to bless a crowned head who makes religious toleration universal through 135 degrees of longitude').[21] Frederick the Great was an agnostic and felt that a man should 'get to heaven in his own way'.[22] It was a feature of the Enlightenment that power should have a secular basis. Even in England, where that idea had started in the 16th century, and where opposition to Catholicism was rooted in fear of political upheaval and the interference of a foreign power in the state rather than in any doctrinal issue, the disabilities on Catholics were repealed in 1829 and on Jews twenty years later.

Religion also had an impact on the development of secular society. This has most famously been stated by Max Weber in *The Protestant Ethic and the Spirit of Capitalism*, in which he made a link between the development of Protestantism and the rise of industrialisation, bureaucracy and nation states governed by the rule of law. In various of his writings Weber charted the rise of the secular nation state and its effect on the course of history: notably in its appropriation to itself of the right to exercise violence against other polities.[23] Schumpeter rejected Weber's notion that capitalism had started only after the Reformation by adducing the example of mercantilism in Italian city-states in the 14th century. He also effectively dismissed Weber as a Marxist.[24] Protestantism certainly reduced the influence and pervasiveness of religion in society, encouraged a more secular form of education, set economic gain as a legitimate activity, and economically benefited those societies that pursued it. In Europe, the 19th century was intellectually dominated by secularisation, and (coincidentally or not) culminated in 1914 in a war of unprecedented barbarism.[25]

The industrial revolution is the key event in economic history. Its causes were numerous, but the idea of a Protestant work ethic has some relevance to it. That industrialisation took place first in Britain was also due to the comparative wealth of the country, obtained from its establishment as a maritime trading nation, which made entrepreneurialism and investment in new technology and processes possible. The English Civil War – one of whose causes, in turn, was the attempt by King Charles I to challenge the Protestant Reformation in England – reinforced that settlement, which was cemented by the Glorious Revolution of 1688. The combination of secularism and dissent that this brought stimulated the growth of a post-feudal middle class, from which the inventors and capitalists of the 18th century were found. After 1685 England also benefited from an immigration from France of Huguenots who fled after the revocation of the Edict of Nantes, many of whom were prominent merchants and traders. In 1656 Oliver Cromwell had agreed to tolerate a group of Sephardic Jews in England, for reasons of state finance, for the first time since their expulsion in 1290.

A new intellectual movement fostered such moral philosophers as Adam Smith who, among other things, furnished one of the blueprints for capitalism. Smith's observation in *The Wealth of Nations* that the pursuit of self-interest benefited society was not especially consonant with Christian doctrine as it had been handed down, however true it was. However, it and other tracts of the Enlightenment that justified capitalism helped stimulate a movement in which wealth creation as an aim was celebrated; a movement that also engaged in acts of philanthropy that by funding housing, schools, museums, municipal government and hospitals improved the living conditions, education and life expectancy of the working class, indirectly fulfilling the Christian exhortation to charity.

Smith was just one of a new generation of philosophers inspired in the centuries immediately after the Reformation by the change of the place of religion in society. In *Leviathan* Hobbes argued that no one else could believe with certainty another's divine revelation and that, therefore, civil power should prevail over religious.[26] This was, as much as anything, made clear to him by the English Civil War. That, and the culmination of the Thirty Years War at almost the same time, signalled a key historical shift from power based on theocratic considerations to power based on secular or material ones. Although it has been argued (most recently by Orlando Figes, in *The Eastern War*) that the Crimean War was sparked by a religious controversy – a dispute between France and Russia about whether the Catholic or the Orthodox church should control Christian sites in Jerusalem – the cause was as much the secular claim by Napoleon III of France's sovereignty in the Holy Land to which Russia, spoiling for a fight over the Ottoman sphere of influence, chose to react strongly. In a secularising century like the 19th there were usually other, less spiritual motivations for conflict and change.

Hobbes was ahead of the main movement of the Enlightenment, which would argue during the later 18th century that reason rather than faith or superstition should provide the legitimacy for exercises of authority. Kant, writing in 1784, argued that enlightenment required man to shake off a sense of tutelage; a century later Nietzsche would more explicitly reject religion and describe the inherent sense of sin as a burden to self-knowledge, wisdom and advancement. Such understandings seemed to remove religious considerations from influencing Western history, and to pave the way for political ideology to determine its course instead. Such a mindset pertained until the end of the 20th century, and when religion once more became a key factor in influencing events, the shock was extreme.

Is the campaign that al-Qaeda has launched against the non-Muslim, and particularly the Judaeo-Christian, world, a new sort of holy war? At the first meeting of those who would form the organisation in October 1988 its founding principles were described as being 'to lift the word of God, and make his religion victorious'.[27] One of its leaders commented, however, that 'Islam is different from any other religion: it's a way of life.'[28] It is debatable whether al-Qaeda is furthering a religious or a political ideology in its programme. Militant

Islam believes that Islam as it is widely practised today has ceased to be Islamic, and needs to be restored to the original form specified by the Prophet. Yet its concentration – so far – on America as the main enemy of true Islam suggests a political motive rather than one of straightforward jihad. Certainly, anti-Americans the world over (whose motivation was purely political and not remotely religious) used the response by America to al-Qaeda's threat to that country to construct a substantial critique of America that, with some help from the American presidency between 2001 and 2008, diminished America's popularity in the world.

Although America is a country in which religion plays a far more important part than in most other Western countries – 92 per cent of those questioned in a poll in 2008 said they believed in God or some other form of supreme being – America's response to the attacks by Islamic fundamentalists was not couched in religious terms.[29] President George W. Bush, speaking that evening from the Oval Office, said that 'America was targeted for attack because we're the brightest beacon for freedom and opportunity in the world.' Having in his opening sentence talked of 'our way of life' being under threat, he added that America's aim was to join with all others who wanted 'peace and security in the world'. There was no mention of the aggressors, in his or his administration's view, being motivated by a religious impulse, and his determination to fight back was justified in secular terms: 'This is a day when all Americans from every walk of life unite in our resolve for justice and peace. America has stood down enemies before, and we will do so this time. None of us will ever forget this day, yet we go forward to defend freedom and all that is good and just in our world.' He did, however, precede that peroration with a quotation from the 23rd Psalm, a clear reminder of the Judaeo-Christian tradition in which he placed himself and his country.

Yet when America led expeditions into Afghanistan, and later into Iraq, it was not ostensibly to defend Christianity. It was, in the case of Afghanistan, to find al-Qaeda operatives and training establishments and remove them. The pretext for the adventure in Iraq was that Saddam Hussein was developing weapons of mass destruction, which turned out subsequently not to exist. In the former operation the aim was to prevent further attacks on America and her allies, protecting a way of life whose priorities were capitalism, prosperity and democracy rather than Christianity. In the latter America's concern was to remove an irritating regime that it had let off the hook twelve years beforehand, during the presidency of George W. Bush's father, and to cement American power in the region. The former aim was achieved, the second disastrously not. What has happened between Islam and the West in the early years of the 21st century is what Huntington defined as 'a fault line war'; he wrote that 'fault line conflicts sometimes are struggles for control over people. More frequently the issue is control of territory.'[30] The activities of al-Qaeda are for the moment provoked by the former, and a desire to control people by converting them to the movement's definition of Islam; that may, however, become more and more concerned with the control of territory, such as the struggle going on today in Pakistan.

America's response to al-Qaeda reflects its secular interpretation of the attacks upon itself. It suggests that it views al-Qaeda as an ideological force that is set upon economic destruction and upon reducing America's quasi-imperial power in the world. The notion expressed at the foundation of al-Qaeda that it was furthering a way of life rather than just a religion seems to support this view. This could be just another conflict using religion as a mask to conceal a naked power-grab. Yet the way of life al-Qaeda seeks to advance is one rooted in the Muslim faith, and it uses an interpretation of the sayings of the Prophet to justify killing infidels, such as in the attacks of September 2001. Although on one level this attempt to shape events seems to have the very modern motivation behind it of enforcing a political system (for that is what the Caliphate can be seen to be) upon unwilling nations, on another the pursuit of conversions to the faith takes us back to the influences on history not merely of the era of the Reformation, or the Crusades, but the seventh century when the Prophet's word was first being spread. It is difficult, once more, to reconcile this perception with the notion that progress is the theme of history. In the second decade of the 21st century, the power of religion to affect international relations remains substantial, and notions of secularisation can apply only to parts of Europe and some of its Europeanised former colonies.

This has even been recognised by some on the centre-left of the British political establishment who, after decades of promoting multiculturalism, have now pronounced that it has failed.[31] The racial and communal agitation it has helped cause has prompted new calls for cultural unity and the acceptance of values embraced by the mainstream – which have more in common with the Christianity that, in its various forms, is not merely the most widely practised religion in Britain, but also underpins much of the British heritage and constitutional settlement. In the rest of the world – Asia, Africa and notably the United States of America – God continues to dominate the outlook of billions of people, and to be a source of tension between them.

Four

– Wealth –

Empires have started for three reasons: to provide or enhance territorial security, as with the Persian and Roman empires; or for reasons of wealth creation, such as the Portuguese, Spanish, Dutch and British empires; or as part of a competition between powers to obtain influence in regions where their rivals were already strong, such as the German and French empires in Africa in the 19th century. Supplementary to this definition is the metaphysical concept of imperialism, the projection of power outside a country without colonisation or necessarily rule, as the Americans have long engaged in and, before 1989, the Soviet Union too. China is developing its own overseas interests in such a way now, notably in sub-Saharan Africa.

The enterprise of imperialism in order to create wealth provides the third recurring theme in the diversion of the course of history. Making money by exploiting the human, material and mineral resources of other lands, or simply enriching first a specific class and then a whole nation, became an attractive option for nations that had made themselves stable and then wished to make themselves rich. Wealth was good for its own sake and had luxurious purposes; but it also helped pay for men and *materiel*, which allowed the enriched nation to become a leading power. Wealth creation also became a by-product of empire-building for reasons of territorial security, as in both the Persian and Roman empires and – thanks to the security of the Silk Road – the Mongol empire of Genghis Khan. The expansion of power not only subdued potential rivals, but it also filled treasuries. Also, the richer a country became, the more it could invest in technology, of warfare and of production.[1]

Even when others have argued that the main theme of history is about progress – be it the improvement of living standards, education, security, tolerance, manufacturing or technology, or more generally the creation of a standard of living that deters people from settling their differences by recourse to arms – these improvements have often been motivated by the desire to expand or secure power of one sort or another, rather than for their own sake or for the sake of altruism or idealism. Societies where philanthropy and disinterest have, at times, become forces have usually only been able to create a climate in which such idealism can flourish as a result of the earlier establishment of power and, through it, the security that enables the creation of wealth.

As soon as the first territorial expansions by the Greeks took place in the eighth century BC, trade began to bring economic dividends. The Romans soon realised that if their power was to increase they had to take a leading role in commerce in the Mediterranean, and that meant exerting control over its trading routes. The Greeks had had to see off the Phoenicians in the seventh and sixth centuries BC, and had failed to do so entirely once the Phoenicians built up Carthage as both a trading centre and a power base. The Carthaginians well understood the link between money and power, and so long as their wealth enabled them to provide a naval threat to the Romans, they were able to impose restrictions on their rivals about where, and with whom, they could trade: such as in the treaty of 306 BC that kept Roman vessels out of the Atlantic and from trading with subjects of Carthage in Sardinia and Africa: this was to ensure that Carthaginian trade with Sicily could be maintained, and that growing Roman naval power was kept at a distance. Like the Phoenicians before them, the Carthaginians lacked a sense of political power. As Mommsen put it: 'As at home the Phoenicians patiently submitted to the oppression of their masters, so also abroad they were by no means inclined to exchange the peaceful career of commerce for a policy of conquest. Their colonies were factories.'[2]

This reluctance to fight meant that more martial powers would overrun their colonies, notably the Greeks. Their ability to generate wealth became compromised by their loss of territory. Eventually, with the assistance of the Carthaginians, they stood up against the Greeks. But this in turn made the Carthaginians ambitious for territory and money. They exerted sovereignty over the Phoenicians and spread across North Africa, and thence around the Mediterranean, whose western area they dominated. Polybius claimed that the First Punic War was simply about the decision of the Romans to secure domination of what was then the known world; what historians have also described as a passion for glory can be seen to be a passion for wealth, both in terms of plunder and in securing trade routes and markets. By driving the Carthaginians out of Sicily – and in being forced to become a great naval power in order to do so – the Romans began the process by which they secured the trade routes of the Mediterranean and saw off commercial rivals. By dismissing these rivals they not only obtained security but also, as if by accident, new provinces and their wealth. Spain, which had been attacked for being the main supplier of Carthaginian soldiers, came to them after the Second Punic War; much of North Africa after the Third. This was not purely to ensure the eradication of the Carthaginians: it was because the agricultural land around Carthage itself was invaluable to an expanding Roman state that had to feed a growing population. This new power, based on territory and wealth, would last more than six centuries.

The conquests of Alexander the Great in the

fourth century BC may have originated in his desire to secure his own position on the Macedonian throne, since the Greek states conquered by his father saw their opportunity to break free: but they soon became motivated by territorial expansion that would bring immense wealth to Macedonia and improve its commercial prospects. His conquests opened the way from Greece into India, central Asia and more distant regions of Africa.[3] As later imperial powers would find, the acquisition of territory and its maintenance in order to extract wealth from it required more and more military power; Alexander's empire did not long survive him. Later, as the power of Rome grew, it diverted much of the wealth of its conquered Greek peoples to itself. As Rome's fiefdoms expanded so too did its trade, wealth and power: and trade with the East of the sort that had hitherto been the province of the Greeks was a symbol of that expansion. Finlay cites the existence of a formal political relationship between Greece and Rhodes in the third century BC as an indication of Rome's recognition of the importance of facilitating and easing the terms of such trade: the wealth it brought was essential for the reinforcement of power.[4]

The existence of wealth in a polity inspires potential conquerors in one of two ways. They can either seek to exploit it to build further trade and prosperity, as Alexander did and, to an extent, the Romans after him, or it can be used simply for plunder by stronger invaders who wish for nothing other than engaging in an asset-stripping exercise. The Goths and Scythians – coming from what is now Germany and Eastern Europe – in their assaults on the declining Roman empire from the late third century AD onwards did just that, to begin with. In the same way that, centuries earlier, the Romans had taken advantage of what they considered the effeminate Greeks to march in and conquer them, so a Roman middle class and aristocracy used to luxury and alien to sacrifice presented a magnificent opportunity to the Goths. As Finlay put it, 'the immorality of the Romans at last undermined the political fabric of the empire'.[5] Diocletian found the empire no longer governable from one centre, and sought to divide it up into four executive operations. That proved divisive, and Constantine undid the reform, unifying the governance from Constantinople, having decided that Rome itself was too inherently corrupt, ungovernable, vulnerable, expensive and potentially disloyal to the emperor: the senate was also hostile to Christianity, and in that respect especially the *tabula rasa* of a new capital was advantageous. While his move separated the Roman in to an Eastern and a Western Empire, its location ensured that the Eastern continued to flourish while the Western was subject to continued vulnerability and decline.

The Muslim world from the eighth century AD

expanded for obvious religious reasons, but also to protect trade routes between Europe and the Far East. The lure of money, not least in its physical, glittering sense, proved compelling to ambitious powers. In the 11th century the Turks moved into India, drawn by accounts of the treasure to be had there. The Spanish conquest of the Americas was not least to secure supplies of silver. The seats of power in many old European polities were on trade routes – London, Paris, Rome – and wealth became the natural concomitant of power even without, necessarily, further conquest. The realisation after the mid-15th century that undeveloped foreign lands contained unexploited natural resources led to a drive for empire by the major seafaring powers of Europe: Portugal to Africa, India and America, Spain to South America, the Dutch to India and the Far East and eventually England to North America and India, followed to both places by the French.

Empire also provided a captive marketplace for the products of industrialised countries, when wealth creation was based upon the ability to sell, at a profit, manufactured goods. These colonies became possessions themselves to be traded at the resolution of European wars, such as the War of the Spanish Succession, the Seven Years War and in the Versailles settlement after the Great War. As wealth creation became more sophisticated, and more reliant on the buying and selling of services, the need for empire diminished. Liberal economists from Adam Smith onwards had demonstrated the indissoluble link between free markets and wealth creation; after an interruption under the Marxist and totalitarian influences of the 20th century, and once the wasting assets of empire had been hived off, the developed world – and then the developing one – was able to return to the path of market economics, with power accruing to those who pursued this doctrine most ruthlessly. Economics as a motivation for war or conflict in modern times could not, however, rival that of ideology, the desire for territory or (with the emergence at the end of the 20th century of militant Islam) religion: societies in which what Carlyle called the cash nexus becomes a predominant consideration understand that more primitive motives to pursue power threaten wealth creation, and they therefore avoid them. While trade and other economic imperatives had been important considerations in the desire for power from the very beginning, the growth from the 16th century onwards of the European empires in the New World put these considerations, for a time, at the forefront.

Claims of 'glory' being the cause of wars are usually a euphemism for the pursuit of wealth, either in land or in more portable forms. When Louis XIV sought *'la gloire'* he sought expansion of his territories and influence; and ostentatious displays of wealth, such as at Versailles, were the symbols of that glory. Wealth could only be guaranteed by security, which, as had been demonstrated by the Romans and others after them, required territorial expansion. 'Ambition and *gloire*' were the only reasons Louis offered for the Dutch War of 1672–8. Britain, having originally resigned itself to a Bourbon king on the Spanish throne, changed its mind during the War of the Spanish Succession for economic reasons. Frederick the Great's determination to expand Prussia did not simply require the territory of Austrian Silesia; it required the wealth of Silesia's natural and other material resources. He was following a precedent set by Sweden and Denmark in their interference in the Thirty Years War a century earlier, which had been largely to obtain economic opportunities in the Protestant territories of the Holy Roman Empire.[6]

In the Dark Ages the Vikings set an example of expansion, or rather intervention in the polities (and therefore the histories) of others, stimulated by the desire for wealth. Their assaults not just on the British Isles but on other areas of Europe were aimed at accumulating wealth, and it has been argued that this was because of the difficulty of developing the agricultural economy in Scandinavia. Their ruthless expansionism had far-reaching consequences: the Normans who invaded England in 1066 had been Danes who had taken that part of northern France in the 10th century. Their motivation, and opportunity, came from the decline of trade in the Mediterranean and on the Atlantic seaboard following the decline of the Roman empire after the fifth century and the rise of Islam in the seventh and eighth. As well as trying to capitalise on under-used trade routes, the Vikings also put their nautical skills to use as pirates and colonists, establishing themselves in the territory of others wherever commercial necessity dictated. Some historians have adduced a religious motivation for the Viking expeditions, namely that the conflict caused by the progress of Christianity through Scandinavia drove many Vikings abroad. If this was of any importance, however, it was very much secondary to the established motivation of identifying new sources of wealth, and wealth that was required as the venture capital for this budding trading operation.[7]

The expansion of power for the sake of wealth rather than security was an aim of Prince Henry the Navigator, son of King John of Portugal and grandson of John of Gaunt, who from his youth in the early 15th century believed it was important for Portugal to explore in order to improve its markets for trade. These trade routes went into the Sahara, but by the 1420s Henry was keen to discover what lay beyond in Africa. King John had conquered Ceuta in North Africa in 1415, neutralising a base used by Barbary pirates who attacked Portuguese shipping and also raided the country's coast to capture people to be sold into slavery. This presented a security issue which Portuguese control of the North African coast would help solve: and Henry had the religious motivation in his desire to explore of wanting to find the Christian African kingdom of Prester John, which was a fiction. However, Henry was above all motivated to find the source of the West African gold trade.[8]

The expeditions he sponsored would be bankrolled by the Portuguese Order of Christ, of which he became governor in 1420, but they had no overt missionary intent. However, when seeking to enrich Portugal by engaging in the slave trade, Henry would justify his expeditions' capture of Africans by claiming he was converting them to Christianity. By the 1440s one of Henry's expeditions had achieved his main aim of finding a coastal route to Lagos, a prime source of gold, slaves and other minerals. This obviated the need to tangle with the Muslim-dominated trade routes through the Sahara. Other expeditions went further south along the African coast, reaching the Cape of Good Hope, and in 1498 Vasco da Gama sailed from Portugal to India round the Cape, opening up one of the most valuable trade routes of all. The last decade of the 15th century is significant in the shift of motive in terms of the main European powers' desire for expansion. Six years before Vasco reached India, Columbus landed in America in 1492. Spain first exploited the

Caribbean in the early 16th century as part of a gold rush – the precious metal was found on Hispaniola (later Cuba) at the very end of the 15th century. The Spanish saw this economically driven conquest also as an opportunity to extend their civilisation and, particularly, the Christian religion, and they did so by force of arms, exploiting the weakness of the ill-defended and shallow-rooted polities they found first in Mexico and then in Peru. By the 1540s Spain had extracted prodigious amounts of gold and silver out of its possessions in America and was using the money better to defend its continental empire, and especially to keep the Reformation at bay in its Catholic provinces in Germany and the Netherlands.

Portugal's possessions on the Indian subcontinent fell victim to overstretch in the early 17th century, with both the English and the Dutch (equally motivated by financial considerations) spotting the opportunity and capitalising on the weakness. The union of the Spanish and Portuguese crowns after 1580 made Portuguese ships and possessions a target for these traditional enemies of the Spanish too, and this stimulated Dutch and English interest in India and the Far East in particular. Portugal's other valuable possession, Brazil, discovered by accident in 1500, lasted until 1822, when it was one part of the succession of South American independence movements. Both these parts of empire enriched Portugal considerably, with proceeds from the spice trade from the Orient and sugar and minerals from Brazil.

English, and subsequently British, imperial ambitions can be analysed in three distinct phases, all of them sharing the motivation of money. The spectacle of the riches coming out of the Americas in the 16th century caused pressure in England for the country to seek to take its share of the wealth; and the same was true of the desire to improve trade with the East. For a time the exploitation of the American resources consisted of state-sanctioned raids by privateers on Spanish and, later, Portuguese ships, using the excuse of Spain's hostility to England's post-Reformation settlement. Eventually the English started to set up trading posts in the Caribbean, and then in the first decade of the 17th century on the American mainland. The instinct behind imperialism in America was more often religious than economic – groups of Catholics or Protestant dissenters took themselves to the New World to be able to have freedom of conscience. The economic potential soon became apparent, and was the driving force for most later waves of emigration to America, whether before or after independence.

The second phase, once the American colonies were lost, was the development of the Indian empire, first through the private means of the East India Company, then (after 1860) the British state. The third was the widespread colonisation of Africa, both for its mineral wealth and, in Egypt, for the control it gave Britain of the Suez route to India and the Far East. The motivations behind both imperial exercises were commercial, though once colonies were established their maintenance and defence became a key part of the strategic considerations of Britain as a power. It meant that in the 19th century Britain devoted much time to worrying about whether Russia would seek to attack and confiscate India. This fear existed purely as a result of the British desire to exploit India for financial purposes. That said, British imperialism, as with all others, had widespread non-financial consequences that altered the course of history. It built Western-style nations in largely unpopulated and primitive territories such as America, Canada, Australia and New Zealand; it spread the English language around the world, including in territories with well-established and sophisticated cultures, such as in India and pockets of China; and it helped spread a distinct system of governance – the Westminster model – to many of its former territories upon independence.

All these things may be traced back to the urge not to be left behind in the rush for wealth in the 16th century, and the understanding that being a great power required money not just to fund defence and security, but also all the other trappings of status. Sometimes the lust for gold encouraged the English to behave as little better than pirates, not

just in the attacks on Spanish treasure ships returning from the New World, but also in the decision in
1665 to start the second Anglo-Dutch War, the purpose of which was to appropriate by force as many
Dutch possessions as possible and to blackmail the
Dutch mercantile class into paying a form of protection money to the English. The attempt failed, and
from then on England (and, after 1707, Britain) felt
that the best way to improve its prosperity was to
avoid having wars.

This was not always possible, and empire became
a cause of war among the imperial powers. The Sev-
en Years War had as its ultimate cause a primitive
desire for territory by conquest in North America,
being the conflict between Britain and France in the
early 1750s. France pursued land in the American
interior, which conflicted with the desire of Britain's
coastal colonies to expand inwards for economic
reasons. The French dispatched more men to North
America to try to secure Quebec – their Canadian
stronghold – and the interior. France needed to be
strong and secure in Europe to be able to expend
blood and treasure on imperial ventures. The weakness of Poland in the 1750s increased the threat of
Prussian expansionism, and the increase of Russian
influence on Europe. This coincided with Frederick the Great's desire to prove to the Austrians that
Prussia was the great Germanic power, something
in which he hoped for France's support against the

Habsburgs. France also wanted to prevent Austria from taking the side of Britain in the colonial struggle. The Franco-Austrian alliance was, however, worn down by Prussia, who forced it to negotiate. Thus it was that the desire for land by conquest, for economic reasons, in the New World caused a re-ordering of the powers in the old. France had no choice but to get out of America, and Britain then turned its attention to Spain. In Europe, the role of supreme power passed from France to Britain, who would eventually be challenged for it by Germany after a 19th century not merely of union, but of powerful industrialisation.[9]

Britain's failure to have control of the Atlantic in the late 1770s over the French, Spanish and Dutch caused them to lose the American War of Independence.[10] It taught a lesson for the later phases of imperial expansion, namely that empires, once conquered, will only be held if the will to rule them is matched by the means to reach them and supply them. It was why the Suez Canal became so important to the British after 1869, in terms of keeping easy access by sea to India. Spain's ignominious share in the naval defeat of France in 1805 spelt the end of its imperial ambitions: Britain, the lesson learned that economic interests are in the end protected only by force or the threat of force, had 'command of the ocean' and was able to exert its power for predominantly economic reasons over the next century or so.

'The Continental System' decreed by Napoleon on 21 November 1806 attempted to retaliate by banning all trade with Britain, and was an early example of the attempted exercise of economic power so familiar in the form of sanctions today. It failed, in that it inflicted more hardship on France and in French possessions; but by this stage few rational decisions were being taken by Napoleon, who in being both a megalomaniac and a nepotist had reverted to a form of medievalism. The abolition the same year of the Holy Roman Empire does, however, underline the secular nature of his pursuit and conception of power. The pursuit of empire by the various powers during the shifting dynamics of the Napoleonic wars was not simply to aggrandise themselves but to prevent the aggrandisement of potential rivals. The theory was that the wealth to be earned from empire would help fund the armies and navies that maintained the power of individual states.

After Adam Smith it finally dawned on polities that wealth could expand, and that one nation's wealth was not necessarily at the expense of another: this too reduced the incidence of war. Britain was chief among the Western powers who by force made Japan open up to trade with them in the 1850s, but this in turn caused Japan to develop economically in order to deal with the West on its own terms. The expansion of England made the country isolationist, caused it to lose interest in Europe and leave Europe to its own devices, but equally gave it an interest in Europe remaining divided. By the early 20th century European wars and tensions were of fatally little account to the British.

The industrial revolution created the wealth that allowed the main European nations to have the armies to secure their expansion: with the inevitable consequences for conflict. When attempting to trade with sophisticated and established civilisations, such as the British had to in India, they had to reach accommodations with local rulers rather than simply impose their will on them. The East India Company, and its translation into the Raj after 1860, was a clear sign of the desire for power being mainly about money, no longer about a religion or the acquisition of territories for their own sake. By the early 19th century, and led by Britain, Europe was the world's main source of capital for investment and trade, an economic fact that largely explains its dominance as an imperial force until the Great War. Modern industry was a phenomenal wealth-creator, and its absence from other older civilisations outside Europe explains why they were left behind.

The pressure on ambitious nations to industrialise also caused conflict. It has been noted in the chapter on Land how one of the motives for Japan's designs upon Korea was that country's mineral wealth, which would be invaluable as raw materials for Japanese industry. The Japanese had a similar motivation in starting their second war with China in 1937. Since the Americans had forced Japan into open trading relationships in the 1850s, Japan had become more and more avaricious. It sought, by force, markets in China, and raw materials from there. This lay behind its invasion of Manchuria in 1931, and was the main motivation for the 1937 war. Economic considerations also affected alliances made because of this war: Britain was supportive of Japan during the conflict because of China's hostility through tariffs against British commerce.

A state's ability to be powerful will always fundamentally be contingent on its wealth. Money pays men to go under arms and pays for the arms they use. Fukuyama has argued that science causes changes in history, not least because of the technology that is developed and acquired by prosperous nations to protect themselves or to aggress against less powerful ones.[11] One could argue that it is not the science itself, but the money that pays for its products and the will to use them that really change history. But it makes the point that it is not merely the pursuit, but the exercise, of wealth that can profoundly affect the course of history.

In pre-industrial times wealth was contingent largely on land, for most of a state's money was earned directly or indirectly from agriculture. Mineral wealth beyond precious metals, too, became important as economies advanced. Frederick the Great took Silesia in 1740, as has been noted, to raise resources for his wars of expansion. Britain and Germany were the first great industrial powers, and it is no coincidence that they led an arms race before the Great War that would become one of the factors precipitating that conflict. Population became even more important in the industrial age than it had been in the agricultural era, because wealth became reliant on industrial output, and until mass production came at the end of the 19th century industry was labour-intensive. Population was also important in the first industrial war – the Great War – because it enabled the great powers to field large armies. In the aftermath of the Second World War the two most populous industrial states on earth – Russia and America – became the superpowers. Now, China has overtaken Russia in wealth and in manpower and is daily becoming a more significant rival to an America that has largely sabotaged its own economy. India, by a zealous attachment to capitalism, threatens to approach America too in the decades ahead, as does Brazil. The uses to which Indian, Chinese and Brazilian funds are put will profoundly affect the course of future events, as will the needs of those countries to protect their economic muscle. There may be a new world order, but people and money are still the essence of a power.

One of the differences between economic imperialism in earlier ages and that of today is that it often required cultural and religious imperialism too: often with conquest taking place that required the spread of the religion and the language of the conqueror, who would, having established his power, then proceed economically to exploit. Secularism has now largely done away with the imposition of religious values by economic conquerors: the dissemination of cultural ones continues to be closely associated with the expansion of economic power. This is true, in different ways, of the export of American values and culture along with McDonalds and Coca-Cola; or the expectation that the nations in Eastern Europe, being Russia's clients for its energy supplies, will accept Russia's cultural and political influence, or at the very least not be hostile to it or seek to undermine Russia's interests by further absorption into the institutions of the West. The desire of liberals in Britain after the slump of the 1930s to create a welfare state – embodied by Beveridge – or indeed the support for health insurance in the 2008 American presidential campaign, were to an extent motivated by a genuine concern on the part of the prosperous to ensure the well-being of the poor. However, there is an element of prudence (or cynicism) on the part of those in power, or seeking it, in this context too. Had Britain's rulers failed to keep the promises to the people of a better life after the Second World War in the same way as they had after the First, the consequences might have been severe – not least risking the establishment of a committed revolutionary leftist party in parliament, as happened in France and Italy. And an American presidential candidate in 2008 who had not at least been willing to make noises about reforming health care would have had little point in staying in the field. Where today the disposition of wealth as a form of power is concerned, there is usually an ulterior motive of pacifying the potential opponents of the powerful, or seeking their democratic support.

Economic power became contingent on three principal factors: the ability to manufacture cheaply but at high quality and high output; the ability to discover and exploit natural resources, or, in default of them, to develop service industries that could earn foreign currency; and the will of polities to allow the growth of free markets and the liberal economy. China at the beginning of the 21st century has gone halfway on these considerations: allowing the enrichment of its workers and entrepreneurs as a form of incentive, but within strictly (state) controlled parameters, and taking advantage of most of the rest of the world's commitment to free trade under the General Agreement on Tariffs and Trade. Its incompletely liberalised economy works for the moment because it is in a seller's market, competing successfully on price with its rivals. If the equilibrium shifts from the supplier to the customer, China may have difficulties with its existing dirigisme. The most important philosophical direction in these regards was given by Friedrich von Hayek and Milton Friedman, applying the intuition of Adam Smith to the modern world, and making the link between growth and liberty. The victory of capitalism over socialism in the battle of ideas during much of the 20th century was not least due to politicians advancing these philosophies, and being able to demonstrate the material benefits of economic and political liberty.

Indeed, those two forms of liberty have gone hand-in-hand. The migration of the poverty-stricken European masses to America during the 19th and 20th centuries allowed the migrants freedom of thought and speech but also increased their economic opportunities and America's economic power. Prosperity became contingent on stability and liberty. The decline of the Ottoman empire was exacerbated by financial overstretch aggravated by a perceived territorial threat from Russia and religious tensions among Christians. Once these factors had been removed after the Great War, Turkey began a slow climb to prosperity. The instability caused by collapsing empires also created conflicts in the desire for influence among the great and expanding powers, which when others decline see the opportunity to acquire more territory or markets, and to garner wealth. The Crimean War was one such conflict, caused by Russia's desire to expand into the Ottoman territories (for strategic as well as economic reasons) and the desire of other European powers, notably the French and British, to stop it. Lenin blamed the Great War on the crisis of capitalism and imperial rivalries in the late 19th century.[12] Schumpeter believed the spur to the Great War was irrational and pre-capitalist, in that proper free market societies would normally see how destructive of wealth wars were.[13] The lesson Austria felt it had to teach Serbia to stop further attacks on its empire took little account of that.

It has already been noted how the Persian emperor Chosroes was spurred by jealousy at the wealth of Justinian to renew war with him in Syria, and to extract tribute in gold that complemented his power. Justinian, though, was willing to pay not simply to secure his territory in Syria, but also to keep open trade routes to North Africa and Sicily and to maintain economic activity. Trade would play a crucial part in the ability of the Greeks to resist the power of the Goths, Lombards and Avars in the seventh and eighth centuries. Positioned as they were on the trade route from India to Rome, Sardinia and Spain, and as an important entrepôt for the Black Sea trade, they won important allies whose own wealth depended upon the commercial power of the Greeks. Greek political stability at a time of disorder in southern Europe generally made other Mediterranean nations dependent on the Greeks for the supply of commodities out of India, such as spices and incense. The

Arabs took their cut in the profits of this trade too, controlling as they did, after the Muslim conquests, the main routes from India through Persia and Syria, and the Red Sea and Egypt; the Greeks had the monopoly of the route through central Asia and the Black Sea. The Greeks also provided value to other nations by their supply of fruit, olive oil and wine, and their manufactured goods such as silk, luxurious clothes, jewellery, arms and ornaments.[14]

The final fragmentation of the Roman empire was caused when one of its key principles – that individual provinces or cities within it should not be allowed to have their own independent systems of defence – was violated to protect the trade of those cities (such as Venice, Genoa and Naples) by allowing them to have armed merchantmen. Finlay makes a point about trade, and its link with liberty, which applies down the centuries, and was most vividly seen in the 20th century in Stalin's Russia, the Soviet bloc after 1945, and Mao's China and its satellites in the Far East. 'An instinctive aversion to the independent position of the commercial classes, joined to a contempt for trade, usually suggests such measures as eventually drive commerce from countries under despotic rule. The little republics of Greece, the free cities of the Syrian coast, Carthage, the republics of Italy, the Hanse towns, Holland, England and America all illustrate by their history how much trade is dependent on those free institutions which offer a security against financial oppression: while the Roman empire affords an instructive lesson of the converse.'[15]

At the beginning of the 21st century, three major new economic powers began to emerge: China, which had developed the art of manufacturing in a way that undercut Western rivals, and which used its rigid political system to enforce high standards sometimes on pain of death; India, which had established a means of undercutting traditional Western service industries as well as setting up a competitive manufacturing base and, like China, exploiting a domestic market of hundreds of millions of consumers; and Brazil, rich in natural resources in a era of rising commodity prices; and having undergone economic reforms aimed at establishing a properly free-market economy. Less certain, but with enormous potential, is Russia.

Humiliated in the early 1990s by the sudden loss of its empire and of its political influence in nearly half of Europe, Russia sits on resources of gas and oil that it can use – and has used – to hold other nations to ransom; but it is an economy riddled with institutional corruption. Russia's short and brutal response to a technical provocation by Georgia, one of its former Soviet socialist republics, in August 2008, showed its willingness to resort to arms to assert itself; a willingness made possible only by its mineral wealth. The aggression was politically useful to the

Kremlin in reminding the world that Russia still had the means to act, albeit against a pygmy of a rival. A chorus of international condemnation stayed Russia's hand after a time: but not so much, perhaps, as the precipitate fall in the price of oil, which removed from Russia the certainty that it could afford not just the aggression, but also going out on a limb in the face of hostile opinion. Wealth, and particularly wealth founded in resources, has become a strong factor in international relations and in the direction of travel for individual states.

Both China and Russia will need to face the conflict of greater wealth causing their people to aspire to freer political institutions. It remains to be seen whether prosperity can continue to grow without democracy, or whether political liberalism is essential if capitalism is to continue to develop. Putin's solution of kangaroo courts and long prison sentences for rich men who seek to challenge his supremacy is hardly an incentive to enterprise. If diplomacy was once the continuation of war by other means, now it is continued by trade. There is the danger, however, that the growing desire for resources could trigger a new drive for territory – such as the Russians beginning a battle for the undersea rights of the Arctic, and Britain seeking to expand her influence in the Antarctic – and that nations starved of resources could pursue aggressive means of obtaining them. The expansion of power through war or by non-martial means has, as has been shown, long been associated with the right to trade.

The pursuit of power, in a world where liberty has been or is being extended, is these days conducted more and more by economic means, with nations being humbled by the economic and cultural might of others rather than by their armies. There are precedents for this stretching back centuries: the British empire was built on such a basis, particularly in Africa and India, with the wealth garnered from the industrial revolution providing the resource to secure territories thousands of miles from home. Now, though, economic conquest requires no occupation, is more subtle, and has become the ultimate measure of a nation's strength and place in the world. The appearance of the icons of American economic power – such as McDonalds and Coca Cola – around the world, even in countries hostile to America, is one symbol of this. In the aftermath of the Second World War, the visibility and success of German exports around Europe and the world – notably from its motor and white goods industries – was a sign of a new paradigm of power, and the same was true with the growth of the Japanese export industry, notably too in cars and electronics. The internet provides another pervasive example. And Russia has been able to exert power over neighbouring countries not by the threat of force, but by the threat of ending energy supplies.

The pursuit of power for the sake of wealth has often been a consequence of power's being pursued for one of the other three motives. However, it can from time to time take centre-stage – and in the last half-century in particular has done so. The inextricable link between capitalism and personal liberty has been an important historical force in the battle against totalitarianism, and it may yet achieve further victories for liberty in Russia, China and parts of Africa. But with the desire to have resources solely to maintain a way of life rather than to become richer likely to become a major force in the next fifty to a hundred years, wealth creation for its own sake may never again be as significant as in recent decades, in the history of which it will come to be seen as the predominant force. Wealth can of course be put to entirely philanthropic uses: but as Marx himself argued, it is usually put to the purpose of extending ownership, and the establishment of economic power whether by polities or individuals is usually a prerequisite to any wholly altruistic use of wealth. Indeed, in a democracy its apparently disinterested use – whether as individual charity or in the form of a welfare state – is often not disinterested at all, but often a means of maintaining order and consent in a secular, post-religious society.

Hitler's social programme in the 1930s was an object lesson in the cynicism of this approach, and had the added bonus of improving the health and fitness of millions who would be called upon to fight for the Wehrmacht.[16] Just as material resources are vital for the maintenance of a polity and its territory, so too do they fund the political movements that drive the implementation of ideologies. Even in the most liberal democracies we see the wealthy buying a share in the political process, such as in the funding of American political parties and the funding of their candidates' presidential campaigns; and (although subject to greater restraint under the law) in the funding of parties' general election campaigns in Britain and in other European countries. In some modern polities, such as Italy, the wealthy actually take over the political process, and become politicians and heads of government.

This used to be common in pre-democratic times and is now once more becoming usual, even in Western Europe. The only difference is that an aristocracy of birth has been replaced by one of money, often self-made. In other polities, where corruption is the established means of conducting politics, participants in the political process find ways of becoming wealthy, and the distinction between financial power and political power is blurred. This has happened in Russia, but also in various African despotisms. The power brought by wealth merely reinforces the truth of the adage that every man has his price; and increasingly shows that wealth can bring power, too. Such a realisation helps put capitalism under attack and gives a new lease of life to critiques by the left that many thought had been left behind with the end of the Cold War, and the triumph of liberty (with its intrinsic belief in free markets) over the command economy. As the next chapter will attempt to show, one of the key motivations behind an ideological approach to politics has been the role of money in a society, and attempts to rectify what is often regarded as its unfair or uneven distribution.

Five

– Minds –

T he influence of religious belief as a motivation to pursue power has, in the modern period, been overtaken by a secular equivalent in the desire to promulgate a political ideology. Since the 18th century the drive for power has often been more nakedly ideological, notably from the beginning of the War of the Spanish Succession, when other European polities decided – and it was an ideological decision – that France and Spain could not be allowed to be linked under one crown. From time to time thereafter nations expressed a desire to reform their own or other polities either by violent or non-violent means, whether genuinely in the interests of breaking autocracy or rule by a foreign power, or as a cover for the seizure of power by non-hereditary despots. This is a theme aired by Machiavelli, picked up by Rousseau before the French Revolution and Paine at the time of American independence, expanded by Marx and Nietzsche, and executed in one sense by the governments of evolving democracies throughout the 19th century in such countries as America, Britain and France, and in another in the 20th century by Hitler, Stalin and Mao. The expansion of democracy at the expense of hereditary or landed power was central to this movement before 1914, though with the rise of dictatorships – often in the name of 'liberty' – frequently coming into conflict with it.

At an extreme, the successful implementation of an ideological programme requires complete co-operation on the part of the society on which it is to be imposed. Democracies are often run by ideologues, who rely on consent for what they do. Otherwise, an ideology may be enforced (whether by communist or fascist dictators) with all the brutality of an inquisition demanding obedience and fearing the lack of it. Notably, undemocratic societies need to control the movement of people in order to retain a population over which to rule and to put at the service of the doctrine: that was why Khruschev stopped a haemorrhage of people over the Hungarian border into Austria in 1956, and built the Berlin Wall five years later. However, ideology has also had its legitimate applications, such as in seeking to spread freedom and democracy. In this sense the liberation movement in South America in the early 19th century was 'ideological', just as was the spread of democratic nationalism in Eastern Europe and in parts of the former Soviet Union after 1989.

In *The Communist Manifesto*, Marx and Engels claimed that 'the history of all hitherto existing society is the history of class struggles'.[1] They contended that the conflict that had always been hidden was now out in the open, the revolutions of 1848 having proved the point. They said that although feudalism had receded, the bourgeoisie who had filled the vacuum had established 'new conditions of oppression'. History was, to them, about a clash of ideologies. In their manifesto, they offered one of their own that would, in the following 150 years, cause seismic changes in the course of history by motivating men and movements to engage in 'struggle'. Industrialisation, the development of new societies in America and elsewhere, and the great growth of trade caused the oppressive bourgeoisie to find new ways of exploiting the proletariat. If the proletariat was to assert itself it had to fight, and fight for the ideological aim of controlling itself, by controlling the means of production and exchange, rather than being controlled.

History would, in Marx's and Engels's view, now be shaped by adherence to ideas, and they defined the central idea of communism as 'the abolition of private property'.[2] The course of history would be altered on the streets, but only after the capturing of minds. Communism was anti-national, or supranational, because as they put it 'the working men have no country'.[3] Such ideas invited visceral opposition from those who had a different intellectual framework, whether as democrats or fanatics of a different stamp, and they duly received it. In the mildest form Western societies, notably America, based themselves on the principle of capitalism, and on capitalism as an essential component of personal liberty. In the most extreme form it provoked an assertion of nationalism, which in its most poisonous form became Nazism.

Nazism also saw history as having been a struggle: in this case between Aryans and Jews. The German *Volk*, in Hitler's view, was the highest incarnation of Aryanism. Jews had no nation and therefore sought to undermine others who did. This meant that Jewishness lent itself easily to the internationalism of Marxism. The enemy became to an extent conflated. When Hitler first went to Vienna as a teenager he recalled that 'my eyes were opened to two menaces of which I had previously scarcely known the names, and whose terrible importance for the existence of the German people I certainly did not understand: Marxism and Jewry.'[4]

Racially based nationalism was the only conceivable bulwark against these enemies, and for Hitler entailed the *Anschluss* finally achieved in 1938: 'one blood demands one Reich'.[5] This developed into the 'the eternal and merciless struggle for the German language, German schools and a German way of life'.[6] Hitler was not, as a young man, a nationalist of the sort that made him an Austrian patriot; he was a pan-Germanist who wanted a union of the German peoples, and for whom an essential part of that union was a hatred of the Jews. Habsburg rule had to be destroyed, and with it the Austrian state, for this to be achieved: for the union he desired could be achieved only under Germany. His nationalism was expressly *Volkisch*, and therefore exclusive. 'The poison of foreign nations gnawed at our nationality,' he wrote.[7] In *Mein Kampf* he caricatures and vilifies Jews and makes them the scapegoat for all society's ills: 'Was there any form of filth or profligacy, particularly in cultural life, without at least one Jew involved in it?'[8] The point about the racial supremacy of the German *Volk* was that it could not proliferate enough; and the more it proliferated, the safer German supremacy was. This promoted the ideology of *Lebensraum*, which in turn would lead Hitler to order the annexation of Poland, Ukraine and Belarus, with the ruthless elimination of the indigenous populations, for resettlement by the *Volk* and the expansion of Germany to the extent where it was an unrivalled world power.

The synthesis Marx and Engels sought was the state achieved by the imposition of their ideology, in which the exploitation of one individual by another and thence of one state by another had come to an end, the revolution having been achieved if necessary by force or by war. Their own thinking owed much to the ideology of the Paris commune, which in the summer of 1792 had finally removed the short-lived constitutional monarchy from France and led to the convention that established a republic with the ideology of liberty, equality and fraternity. As Marx and Engels would seek to do, the Girondins of 1792 wanted to export their revolution to other countries; which led them to start a war on Austria (homeland of the Queen, Marie Antoinette) and then Prussia, both of them monarchies controlling adjacent territories.[9]

Stalin seems to have taken this principle very much to heart in 1939, when the pact with Hitler allowed him to communise the Baltic States until Hitler overran them in 1941, and again from 1944 to 1991. He took the same attitude to those countries within the Soviet bloc after 1945, his determination to secure the revolution causing heavy-handed interventions in both Poland and Czechoslovakia: and his heirs took a similar view in Hungary in 1956, Czechoslovakia in 1968 and Poland in 1981. Hitler, however, had done just the same with the European countries his forces overran between 1938 and 1945. These were changes to the course of history willed by ideological considerations; they were designed to impose a system not just of politics, but of thought, on the people subjected to that will.

The origins of this long precede either Marxism or Nazism, and indeed Girondism. From the time of the Reformation onwards, ideology steadily supplanted religion as a motive for the pursuit of power. In some societies religion and politics are or have recently been linked – such as in the connection between Toryism and High Church Anglicanism in England, the religious right's influence over the Republicans in America, or the church's opposition to Marxism in Eastern Europe after the Second World War. In other societies politics has to some extent eliminated religion, not least thanks to Marx's and Engels's denunciation of it in their *Manifesto*. However, the process of secularisation began on the left in the 18th century, with one of its first prophets being Rousseau and another being Thomas Paine: and it was fed by the suave atheism of Gibbon. The expansion of secular interests in Europe, notably the desire of nations in a rivalry for power between 1700 and 1989 to extend influence whether on that continent or in the wider world, finally pushed religious considerations to one side. This is evident in the War of the Spanish Succession, but more forcibly in the ambitions of Napoleon, which in 1806 put an end to the Holy Roman Empire; and in those of Bismarck, which established the first modern economic power on the mainland of Europe.

This shift of the nature of power in the old world was institutionalised at three great events over a hundred years: the Congress of Vienna, the Congress of Berlin, and the Versailles conference. Arguably it can be traced back to the early 18th century, when the British involvement in the Wars of the Spanish Succession was not merely to further the cause of Protestantism – this was only a decade or so after the Glorious Revolution – but to avoid a universal monarchy, or power bloc, on the continent. This was fundamentally a territorial question, not a religious one, and it soon became ideological, touching on the whole question of the balance of power. Hitler repeatedly protested in *Mein Kampf* that he 'understood' history, by which he seems to have meant that he felt what he knew of history allowed him to elevate racially founded nationalism into an ideology.

However, ideology – a systematic scheme of ideas used to justify a particular course of policy – has been present in decisions about the exercise of power for as long as history has been recorded, and has caused changes in the course of history. Thucydides argued that 'the growth of the power of Athens, and the alarm which this inspired in Sparta, made war inevitable'.[10] This can be defined as a defence of honour; but it can also be defined as a defence of sovereignty and what would, after the birth of nations, be seen to be ideological nationalism. What Lebow calls 'the need to defend Spartan values and identity' is a clear statement of ideology, and is similar to Hitler's own remarks about his being motivated by the need to defend the German way of life.[11] Another consequence of the Peloponnesian War was to provoke a sense of Pan-Hellenism through recognition of a common Greek culture; and it was argued, not least by Aristophanes in his *Lysistrata*, that this 'nationalist' impulse could be used to have a final reckoning with the Persians. This was also an early sign of the territorial impulse, for it was suggested that Greeks could then colonise Persian territory not for security reasons – for the threat of Persian force would have been eliminated – but for reasons of aggrandising the state.

Organised religion was an obvious target for revolutionaries because of its use by the established governing class in Europe as a means of social control: 'As the parson has ever gone hand-in-hand with the landlord,' Marx and Engels wrote, 'so has clerical socialism with feudal socialism.'[12] The pursuit of power by ideologues then had to enshrine an ideology to trump religion and provide a new faith for its followers. This can be traced in Europe from the French Revolution, the revolutions of 1848 and the Russian Revolution of 1917 onwards. In the aftermath of the entrenchment of the first Marxist state in Russia after 1917, it was inevitable that an opposing creed, in various forms, should be developed to oppose Marxism's spread in countries where inner turbulence created the potential for a shift of power: hence the rise of fascism in Italy, Germany and Spain. In the period from 1905 to 1989 there was a prolonged struggle between conflicting extremes of ideology over which would prevail, struggles that would typically begin in civil war and end with international conflict. Ironically for the ideologues, the victory after 1989 appeared to be for a non-extreme, democratic, liberty-based form of politics: it is what provoked Fukuyama to write *The End of History*, a clever book that now, as has already been shown, seems to have been somewhat premature.

Before this triumph of consensual politics the pursuit of ideology was rarely, and then often accidentally, coupled with democracy: it was usually conducted by force of arms and dictatorial imposition. By the mid-20th century religion as a source of contention in international relations was often non-existent: the driving force in history had become that of an ideology being carried forward by doctrinaire fanatics and on subject peoples, who were forced to live according to its tenets and its entirely secular values, and under the threat of substantial military power to enforce continued obedience. Some of this necessitated territorial control, or the threat of it. When Hungary in 1956 or Czechoslovakia in 1968 threatened to break with Soviet doctrine, tanks came in; and when agitation began in Poland in the early 1980s the Soviet-backed regime there used its own heavy hand, in declaring martial law, to avoid a more direct intervention. Territory has, as has been discussed, often been sought in order to provide security. Soviet hegemony in the Eastern bloc from 1945 to the early 1990s did not have as its purpose the protection of Soviet territory, but the protection of the ideology it had forcibly exported to them. To some extent, Hitler had taken this view too. Just as Stalin executed or deported those who opposed his rule and his doctrines in the countries annexed by Sovietism – notably the three Baltic states incorporated into the Soviet Union after Hitler's defeat – so too did Hitler view the occupation of other lands as an opportunity to deport and murder the supposed Jewish and Marxist enemy, to protect not so much the physical entity of the German Reich as its system of beliefs.

In the early modern period, as societies became richer and more educated, so philosophers turned their minds more and more not just to the nature of power, but to the systems of maximising and controlling it. In *The Prince* Machiavelli made the argument, in the 16th century, about the ruthlessness a ruler needed to display if he was to retain power. Whatever Machiavelli's personal characteristics as a courtier, his philosophy reduced the importance of conventional morality in the exercise of power, arguing as it did that in the interests of the stability of the state almost any act of ruthlessness could be contemplated. Machiavelli, unlike many other philosophers, political scientists and historians, had no qualms about identifying the fundamental motivation of the pursuit of power in conditioning the actions of states and the great men who controlled them, however vulgar such an admission might have been.

Hobbes justified, or at least described the

inevitability of, such a system of rule. His was a view in which society had alternatives laid out before it: that of the 'state of nature', anarchy, in which the devil takes the hindmost and the powerful eliminate the weak, or that of the ordered society, in his view ruled by an absolutist sovereign, where everyone had a place and in which rules were enforced and obeyed.[13] There was a further option, which was democracy: though as late as the 19th century Carlyle, in attacking plans for a second Reform Bill, equated this with a determination by a society not to have proper leadership.[14] However, from the Reformation onwards there began a shift away from despotism or oligarchy and towards democracy, even though despotism put up a tremendous fight to survive and, in certain areas of the world, still does.

The shift from its being usual for power to be controlled by an elite, to its being usual for power to be controlled by the masses, is the most important consequence of the intervention of ideology in the course of history. Democracy is often presented as an alternative to ideology, which is used by some only to describe versions of totalitarianism, but the notion of mass participation in politics is itself an ideology: and its consequences in history are therefore of ideological origins. In Europe and then in other areas of the world settled by Europeans this movement began with the undermining of the universality in Christendom of the Catholic church. As the power of the church was broken by adherence to an idea, so a social structure that had been implicit in and upheld by the traditional religion was put under threat. With the repudiation of the idea of the divine right of kings came the beginning of the end of the notion of deference as a means of ordering Western societies. The English civil war and the Glorious Revolution of 1688 both exemplified this, and the former was in its way a precursor of both the American and French revolutions. Power had been vested in institutions controlled by important individuals: whether a Pope or, locally, archbishops and bishops, or in secular contexts kings and princes. A reinterpretation of the Bible with the coming of Protestantism, and the later shifts to nonconformity, secularism and atheism, fed the movement to democracy. Whereas power had in the past been the province of magnates, and used to secure their own privileges, a share in it was now demanded by the masses, until the point where their nominees executed it on a renewable popular mandate.

In the late 16th and early 17th centuries the emancipation from Spain of the seven provinces that became the Dutch republic showed the inevitable desire for independence and self-determination in developed societies that had been placed under foreign rule. Two centuries later Paine, Rousseau and Marx argued the rationale for the masses to wrest power from small governing elites, and to an extent suggested the means of doing so – either through democracy, or if consensus could not be obtained, by violent revolution. Rousseau took up from Hobbes and Locke an idea of a 'social contract' between rulers and the ruled, but in his view the rulers had to act within the bounds of a 'general will', not impose their will on the ruled. Marx's ideas of workers' domination relied on a weak state, post-Christianity and internationalism; some of those who flew under his flag (notably Lenin) enforced the last two considerations by ignoring the first, with the state as a means of repression to organise labour and enforce the rest of the Marxist programme. For the potentially powerful, all idealism is negotiable.

Neither the American revolution nor the French settled the argument between despotism and democracy, and nor did the liberation of much of South America from Spanish rule. America had been a nation founded in the ideological pursuit of liberty: the original English colonists in the early 17th century had sought freedom of conscience and escape from forms of absolutism. Its federal constitution of 1789 is widely represented as an embodiment of enlightenment values. It would be over seventy-five years before those values would be properly advanced throughout the Union, with the abolition of slavery after the civil war. The ideas of equality expressed by the constitution would not finally be achieved until after the civil rights movement of the 1950s and

1960s, a powerful ideology of racism lingering in parts of America for a century or more after the civil war. That war, between 1861 and 1865, was on one level an ideological war over the principle of human rights; for the slave-owners of the American south it was also an economic question, as they saw Lincoln's aim of ending slavery as an attack on their assets.

What happened in France was a further spur to Prussian nationalism under a king and, ultimately, German unification under a Kaiser, itself an even more powerful form of ideological nationalism. Napoleon himself recognised the power of hereditary monarchy and the imperial theme and tried to embody his own power in it by declaring himself Emperor. Following his defeat the traditional systems of government – autocracy or an elite with more or less untrammeled power – reasserted themselves throughout Europe. The Napoleonic wars were, though, essentially wars of ideology: not so much for the Burkean reason that revolution in France might lead to one in England, nor even for the security threat that would be posed to England by a French-dominated continent, but because traditional systems of power, such as monarchy, could be uprooted and replaced by new systems.[15] This was what the Directory sought to do after the execution of Louis XVI: in time, the attempt at a new system failed. Napoleon established what was effectively a new monarchy, usurping the old. In doing so he demonstrated his recognition that his exercise of power depended upon the acknowledgement of his legitimacy by those over whom he wished to rule, and that the ruled were still prepared to accept government only in certain prescribed forms. It was not until Russia in 1917 that evolution was pushed aside by revolution with any lasting effect, when what came to be defined as legitimacy was acquired by ruthless use of force.

Lafayette arranged for France to declare war on Austria in April 1792 to strengthen his own position in France. Danton's ambition towards the weak collection of states in Italy in 1793 was ideological, designed again to export revolution, as well as seeking territorial conquest for its own sake to aggrandise the new France and make the revolution appear more formidable. In November and December 1792 the French government issued decrees promising assistance to any revolutionary movement in any other country that sought to overthrow its government.[16] It is also true that the Directory wanted France kept at war to inspire nationalism and support for itself, and to distract attention from shocking domestic conditions.

Britain entered the war in 1793 to preserve 'peace'.[17] In other words, it wished to preserve the established order and to prevent the further export of revolution. It was also nervous of Russian expansionism at the expense of Turkey, and Prussian expansionism into Holland. Its motivation was thus both ideological and pragmatic. Something similar was true in 1914 (though one must not discount British determination to defend the neutrality of Belgium, as it had been obliged to do by provisions in the Treaty of London of 1839), and would have been so in 1939 had not a clear potential threat to British sovereignty been established by the Germans. In different parts of Europe during the 19th century the desire to defend the established order manifested itself on several occasions and took various forms. Revolutions in both 1830 and 1848 were opposed by *anciens régimes* for ideological reasons and out of self interest.

Once the attempts to democratise the social order of Europe had failed in 1848, reaction became even more entrenched. 'I shall not allow Austria, the inconvenient, intriguing Austria, to be attacked by the Revolution, without drawing the sword on her behalf, and this from pure love of Prussia, from self-preservation,' Frederick William IV of Prussia declared in 1854.[18] When Italy was unified in 1861 it was under a monarchy, and the King of Prussia became Emperor of Germany when Bismarck engineered the unification of that nation a decade later. With strong competing nations in Europe the concept of the balance of power became ever more crucial if peace were to be maintained, which worked until one nation – Germany – decided that its wealth and population merited its being the superpower. As Sir Edward Grey observed in 1908: 'After a big war a nation doesn't want another for a generation or more. Now it is 38 years since Germany had her last war, and she is very strong and very restless, like a person whose boots are too small for him. I don't think there will be a war at present, but it will be very difficult to keep the peace of Europe for another five years.'[19] The power of the ideology of nationalism knocked the traditional agreement about the balance of power sideways.

The nations of Europe had a modernised, industrialised model as their aim; the ideological conflict in such polities would come first between capitalism and communism, then between authoritarian fascism and communism, with capitalism and social democracy fighting, for many years fruitlessly, to give a political lead from the centre ground. Marx and his disciples felt that the new wealth of Europe was made by exploitation of the working class; and was then used to arm to fight wars in which the proletariat, as pawns of the moneyed classes, were mostly killed. At another extreme Nietzsche and his followers saw the (albeit limited) concessions made by the Kaiser to the bourgeoisie of the Second Reich as simply decadent, and destructive of the power of Germany.[20] Before the Great War the ideological quarrel was not between those who favoured autocracy and those who favoured collectivism; it was between autocrats and democrats. Within fifteen years of the Armistice of 1918 the three main defeated powers of that war had either become dictatorships or were, in Austria's case, struggling in vain to avoid becoming part of one. The democratic ethos of the victorious ones – Britain, France and America – was implicit in their reluctance to engage in expansionist or aggressive policies after 1918. Only Italy, of the victorious powers, chose the other option, with catastrophic results.

The 1914–18 war was the debacle of the old imperial powers and their ruling orders: it even marked the beginning of the end of the international power of one of the victorious democracies, Britain, with America determined, from the time of Versailles onwards, to end British imperial power and have European power contained within Europe. Nietzsche's idea that the 'will to power' was fundamental to the desires of many men picked up Machiavelli's theme of 300 years earlier, and laced it with Schopenhauer. This, and his denial of such things as a universal morality and the existence of God, helped inspire a new generation of ruthless despots. In *Zarathustra* Nietzsche specifically depicted the will to power as the fundamental human instinct, and attacked Christianity as being a brake on action.[21] This justification of amorality was the final encouragement to extreme ideology, whether Nazism or Communism. Max Weber's analysis of the typology of power also gave instruction to dictators: he outlined the possibilities of the 'charismatic leader', a type personified later by Lenin and Hitler.[22] Weber also contradicted Marx, predicting that socialism would lead to the strengthening and not the decline of the state, and he was proved right; but then Marx was only ever an excuse for Marxist dictators, who have ever shown the need for a strong state to provide a resource for medieval-style patronage, thereby allowing them to maintain their personal power.

There had been a revolution in China in the winter of 1911–12, not precipitated by one of the new ideologies, but by an ethnic grievance dating back centuries: the wish of the vast majority of Chinese – the Han Chinese – to rule themselves, and not to be ruled by the minority Manchu Chinese of the Qing dynasty. No sooner was this revolution, provoked by a sense of atavistic nationalism, undertaken than another began: the agitation of the left in China, inspired by the success of communists in Russia. Sun Yat Sen, the leader of the republic of China, had sought help from the Soviet Union to suppress warlordism in some of his provinces. The Soviets operated a dual policy of supporting both Sun, in his attempts to unify China, and the nascent Communist Party of China. A civil war began in 1927 that was interrupted only by the Japanese attacks on China. After Japan's defeat in 1945 it resumed, and the Kuomintang were defeated by the Communists.

The ideology of the left had claimed its most populous prize.

The revolution in Russia, which precipitated the end of that country's involvement in the wider conflict that had begun in 1914, ushered in not merely an exportable ideological rule that was attempted, over the next decade or so, in other European countries; it also helped create the rival (though in its belief in central control and hostility to personal liberty and democracy, not the polar opposite) force of fascism, in Germany under Nietzsche's indirect influence. Ideological revolutions also allowed individuals to assert control on the pretext of advancing their doctrines just as hereditary princes had, half a millennium before, asserted theirs by relying on divine right; and, as in the case of divine right, the new ideologies could be used to shore up the personal power of an individual and the clique with whose help they ruled: Hitler's Germany, Stalin's Russia and Mao's China were all examples of this.

While a case can be made by the purveyors of all ideologies – whether communism, fascism or even the ideology of democracy – that their way is the way best to secure the rights of most of the people, that is not what historians, or those who read history, should see as the only reason for their actions. Hitler promised to make the German people strong; Stalin promised to give all under his yoke an equal share in society; democratic leaders promise to execute the will of the people as expressed through the ballot box. In each case a calculation has been made about what means in that particular polity is going to be most effective at obtaining and retaining power: idealism may indeed sometimes come into it, but usually pragmatism, and an estimation of what the seeker of power can get away with by exploiting the feelings of those he would rule over, is at the heart of the matter.

The imposition or aggressive pushing of ideology leads to one of the more contemporary themes and motivations in the ideological pursuit of power, which is to seek power as a means of securing liberty and the rights of individuals. Although quickly bastardised, this intention lay behind the French and Russian revolutions: but, ironically, emancipation led quickly to terror and control. The pursuit of liberty in Western society traces itself back to acts of resistance to conquests, whether in the Peloponnesian Wars, after conquests by Rome, the Norman invasion of England or English attacks on France. In England, the civil pressures that led to Magna Carta, de Montfort's parliament and the peasants' revolt are early manifestations of the desire for political liberty. It becomes even more organised and widespread when the force being resisted is religious rather than martial, and this is clear from the time of Lollardry and the Reformation onwards. The liberty to practise freedom of thought in religion was the first great emancipation movement. It gave rise to Martin Luther, the Pilgrim Fathers, the birth of America: but it also was one of the distant causes of the Civil War in England, and the creation of the Dutch republic. The American War of Independence, the abolitionist movement in slavery, the revolutions of 1848, and the pursuit of Italian nationalism were all examples of this pursuit of personal power, and its acquisition from the state, in a more secular context. The creed has had, however, its greatest flowering since 1945, first in opposition to any resurgence of Nazism and other forms of fascism, then in the Cold War and the growth of the dissident movement. It was most clearly seen in the counterpoint of America and the West, with their values of the growth of the individual and personal human rights, and the Soviet bloc, with its emphasis on the state and the individual as the controlled servant of the state.

The rise of an educated or intellectual class, which came more quickly with the creation of wealth and the liberalisation of thought in northern Europe after the Reformation, inevitably caused the questioning of established orders, especially those that (in increasingly secular times) claimed the divine right to rule. The French Revolution was partly precipitated by the new currents in thought in the 1770s in France, which was now becoming prey to the Enlightenment; and partly by the humiliation of the Bourbons in failing to keep France's formerly great position in the world, and ensuring that they and the aristocracy did not share in the hardships of the French people in a time of national impoverishment. France's desire to be great again spurred it on to conquest. The revolution gave rise to the *Code Napoléon*, which in its effective nationalisation of law and abolition of privileges of birth itself was a strong form of ideology. Bonapartism betokened a new embodiment of French influence and greatness. Napoleon wanted Egypt as an empire for its own sake, but also to control access to India and challenge British influence there. The wars that followed allowed the British, in their victory, to acquire many more overseas territories from the French. Napoleon's attempt at European dominance after Austerlitz ended in collapse: mature sovereign states, used to having their own power, resented his conquest and the imposition of his system. The sheer extent of his lands made governing them extremely difficult, militarily and bureaucratically. His final attempt to deal with the threat posed by Russia was fatal. The 'concert of Europe', brokered at Vienna in 1814, helped stave off a Europe-wide war for the next hundred years by a voluntary agreement to limit power in relation to each other by the great powers: Austria, Britain, France, Russia and Prussia.

The chapter on Land has discussed territory as a motivation for war in the context of aggression or expansion. When those aggressed against or simply annexed seek to restore sovereignty that becomes an ideological question, and one of nationalism. The ideology of nationalism can be toxic, as the Germans showed before 1914 and 1939, or as the Russians have from time to time showed since the beginning of the 21st century. For Germany in the era of Bismarck and Kaiser Wilhelm II there was a determination to become a world power – to impose a *Pax Germanica* – which the Kaiser's advisers told him required victory in a European war, preferably at the expense of those who implemented the *Pax Britannica*. This first required the establishment of an ideological German nationalism, born out of Prussian nationalism, before it could be imposed upon a wider stage. The *Pax Americana* that prevailed after 1945 came as a result of others starting a war, but the opportunity to establish it was seized by the United States, with mixed results and, inevitably, inviting accusations of imperialism and arrogance. In its promotion of 'the American way' and its inherent values, it was nakedly ideological.

However, nationalism can also be benign, and take the form of a desire for self-determination rather than expansion. This happened in the Americas against the English and the Spanish. It happened in the Austro-Hungarian empire as Czechs, Slovaks, Slavs and, fatally, Bosnians sought to throw off the imperial yoke. Most recently it happened in Eastern

Europe and the former Soviet Union, where satellite states rid themselves of the influence of Moscow, and lands incorporated into the Soviet Union asserted their right to self-determination. What Latvia, Estonia and Lithuania did in the early 1990s, or what Poland did after Versailles, was as ideological in its pursuit of nationalism as anything the Germans did; but it had nothing like the same intentions. What all these aspirations to statehood have in common with aggressive, expansionist nationalism is that they have all required a mass movement behind them, and the harnessing of minds – whether in rebel movements or, in Hitler's case, to mount a successful election campaign. Hitler was motivated by Germany's lack of standing after Versailles, and wished to rectify it: but his motivation was not a sense of slighted honour, but of ideological nationalism laced by the sting of inferiority.

In the 20th century a war prompted largely (as the Marxists argue, with some reason) by economic rivalries after the century of peace brought in by the Congress of Vienna was followed by two international wars of ideology: the first, from 1939, was the result of Hitler's determination to pursue aggressive nationalism through the medieval means of taking additional territory by conquest, tearing up the diplomatic blueprint settled by the League of Nations, to which the world's democracies (except America) subscribed. The second was the Cold War, in which two heavily armed and ideologically opposed blocs faced down each other for forty-five years, until the desire for liberty and democracy prevailed. There were also numerous civil wars of ideology: notably the war in Spain between 1936 and 1939, and in China after 1945.

Trotsky read both Schopenhauer and Machiavelli; the former taught him that winning, however it was accomplished, was all that mattered.[23] This may explain the ruthlessness with which Trotsky exercised power when in charge of the Red Army at the Revolution. He dismissed the plays of Ibsen because of their obsession with the fate of individuals. As a Marxist, he was concerned only with collective solutions.[24] He also drew inspiration from the French Revolution, though disdained the utopianism of the Jacobins while admiring their zeal.[25] He sought a dictatorship of the proletariat engaged in permanent revolution. Lenin wanted this to include the poor peasantry; but Trotsky was interested only in the industrial proletariat. Stalin, by contrast, became more obsessed with the retention of his personal power, using alleged breaches of the ideological rule as his excuse to remove dissidents and rivals, real or imagined.[26]

It was not until the defeat of fascism in 1945 that the centrist doctrines of social democracy and capitalism were able to have a straight contest with communism. By the force of their ideas, rooted in liberty and freedom, they were able, after forty-five years, to win: with liberalisation in China, the end of murderous totalitarian regimes such as that of Pol Pot in Cambodia and the expansion of democracy into the former Soviet bloc, the determination to exercise power by controlling the lives, industry and thought of a whole population is now confined only to marginal relics of communism such as North Korea and Cuba and closed authoritarian societies such as Burma. It still exists, in another form, in some of the despotisms of the Islamic crescent, and it is the nature of that exercise of power that provides the greatest philosophical and security challenges for the world in the immediate future. In the rest of the world, those who wish to exercise power understand that they need the approval of electorates to give them legitimacy. Mostly this is real, sometimes it is pastiche – as in contemporary Russia. The modern age, however, dictates that rule has to be legitimated by the ballot box. This is not a sign that the political class has given up power: it has just learned that it must go through certain procedures to earn the right to exercise it. Even then, the ballot box only legitimates rule within the polity. Old-fashioned imperialism, expansionism and intervention – such as America's in the Middle East since the attacks on it in 2001 – risk obloquy because of their violation of the new order.

Schumpeter's belief that social democracy and

not revolution would be the reaction against capitalism has largely been proved correct; as has his idea that democracy was an opportunity for politicians to manipulate voters and get their own way. Also, his view that capitalism would cause an educated class to grow (which had been the case in Europe since medieval times) has been proved true, which has meant wealth has expanded, wars have been avoided, and those who wish to run despotisms try to remove all the intellectuals. His philosophy stands in contrast to Francis Fukuyama's belief that Western liberal democracy has triumphed, something that Islamic fundamentalism, the growth of China as a power and the growing restlessness of post-Soviet Russia seem to call into question.

Samuel Huntington argued that modernisation can cause stresses that lead to violence, and that democratisation needs to be managed: something that can be seen to have happened in Brazil, and may yet have to happen in China. As we have already noted, he argued that clashes in future would be between civilisations rather than ideologies. Before one assumes that the conflict between militant Islam and America and its allies after the attacks of 11 September 2001 supports this, one needs always to define how far the motivation of al-Qaeda is religious, and how far ideological. The distinction, as discussed earlier, is not so easy to make as might be hoped. Even after the great clash of ideologies supposedly finished with the end of the Cold War, however, the force of ideas is still strong in the world. A principled opposition to America both as an idea in its own right and as an entity is what passes for one of the world's great ideas, though it derives from the age-old creeds of anti-capitalism and anti-imperialism. So is environmentalism, which subordinates all other considerations to that of the preservation of the planet, and often on a less-than-scientific basis. Perhaps it is that whenever a bad idea is finally defeated a new one must rise in its place, in order not to give the victor a clear run. And those who originate, or borrow, those ideas will always seek the power to enforce them, and to impose them upon others.

Six

– Future –

Fukuyama was perhaps premature in contending that there had been some sort of resolution in history, with the 'logic of modern science' and the 'desire for recognition' leading inevitably to the collapse of tyrannies.[1] Perhaps, in his determination to read the last rites over Karl Marx, he neglected to note that there was more than one potential opponent to the American, or liberal democratic, way of doing things.[2] It is ironic that he should wish to dispatch Marx, because his own belief in history as progress is Marxist as much as it is, in the English context, Whiggish. This 19th-century optimism seems profoundly out of place now. Strife between civilisations and financial collapse have brought new perspectives on the world, and reminded us that the pursuit of power by individual polities, for all the traditional reasons, is a constant. Nothing is yet settled; and probably it never will be.

In the early 21st century it remained clear that the achievements of democracy were not recognised by all civilisations; and, indeed, were challenged by forces in the world sufficient to ensure that the acceptance of democracy as the basis for the world's future would not be automatic. Conceptions of history such as Fukuyama's arise in ages of plenty and of optimism – Macaulay, the godfather of this creed, developed it at a time of the seemingly unlimited expansion of British power and prosperity. The worst global economic downturn for eighty years, and the threat to Western values offered by militant Islamists, have returned the world to a state of pessimism. One feature of that pessimism should be our understanding that the pursuit of power, by whatever means, is an eternal phenomenon, and eternally destabilising.

Democracy itself, in the first decade of the present century, showed its vulnerabilities and opened itself to challenges. The decision by America to pre-empt, or supplant, the United Nations and lead an invasion of Iraq in 2003 was not how modern democracies were supposed to behave. This exercise cannot be compared with the first Gulf War of 1991: then, Iraq had undertaken an act of aggression against Kuwait; Kuwait appealed to the world for help; the world helped under the agreed auspices of the United Nations; when it had achieved its war aim of doing what the Kuwaitis had asked, it went home. Democracies are entitled to defend themselves and their values against provocations: however, the basis upon which the 2003 adventure was justified at the time was quickly shown to have been unstable. No evidence has yet been found that a threat to the security either of America or the rest of the Western alliance was presented by the continuance of the tyrant Saddam Hussein in power. What followed therefore appeared to be an exercise in American imperialism – the imposition of that civilisation's values upon another, in precisely the sort of conflict predicted by Samuel Huntington. The exercise of power in extending the hegemon's values was done through the ancient means of the control of territory.

It has also been an underpinning of belief in liberty that its prevalence is required for the operation of a free market, and that such a free market is the means by which the prosperity of a society is maximised. [3] This notion is challenged especially by China, where growing prosperity is achieved despite the absence of democratic values. By ignoring many of the add-ons that go with democracy in the West, such as employment laws and health and safety regulations, China can undercut those economies in which these social considerations are deemed essential. Furthermore, the near-collapse of the West's banking system because of regulatory failures and the perceived decadence of over-remunerated capitalists has offered an extra challenge to the supposed supremacy of that means of conducting economic and political life.

Fukuyama also failed to predict the differing approaches that the most important parts of that liberal consensus – America and Europe – had to furthering the new orthodoxy, or so-called new world order, a division that would offer opportunities to the enemies of liberalism. When the West had a common enemy during the Cold War it was relatively easy (though not inevitably so) to reach accord on matters of policy. Once the common enemy evaporated there was much more room for debate among the Western allies about goals for the future. To Europe, the new post-Cold War orthodoxy would be furthered by the liberal means of enabling a victory of ideas after a period of persuasion and argument. To the Americans the new order would be imposed, if necessary, by force, and America would be the leading power in doing so. Indeed, America before the events of 11 September 2001 saw itself (following the collapse of the Soviet Union) as the only world power, the unquestioned power for the future, and one that by wealth and geographical situation was invulnerable either to economic or physical assault. History shows that no such assumption, though similar have often been made, is reliable.

Europe after the Second World War identified the ideology of the nation state as the source of conflict in so many of its wars since the Treaty of Westphalia. This was because of the desire of nations from time to time (and notably, since the mid-19th century, Germany) to overturn a balance of power and to assert the values of their own particular nationalisms. As a counter to this ideology it developed a variant of its own, which has become just as powerful an ideology in its way: supra-nationalism. It has sought through the European Union to begin a project of eliminating nations and nationalism from the ideas of Europe, and forging instead a common European polity. Power will always remain a driving force: supranationalism is an attempt to reduce and eliminate the conflicts that arise in the pursuit of power, not least by establishing common systems of territory, markets and values, and (in the European context) doing so in a predominantly secular way. This is one model of civilisation; it is challenged both by the notion of Islam, which remains theocratic in its driving force, and by the rise of other fundamentalisms, such as among Christians in America.

The Treaty of Lisbon, ratified in 2009, was the latest and most significant part of the diplomatic process used to further supranationalism, with its provision for the European Union to have its own foreign minister and foreign policy. A single currency and economic policy were already extant, though do not – yet – include all 27 members of the EU. Although in Huntington's view the West is a common civilisation, one of the driving forces behind European integration has been to create a power bloc capable of matching that of America. Rivalries and differences are inevitable, and not just between these two regions in the same civilisation. They are also happening within Europe, because of the discrete histories, identities and ethnicities within the European Union, and may yet happen in America, where a gulf is already visible between the 'liberal' east and west coasts and the more conservative 'middle America'.

It is believed by European idealists that Germany can become, within the European Union, something like Texas, with a definite identity of its own but also with a sense of belonging to something with a common future. However, the historical sense of the various European peoples, with distinct national identities, ethnicities and atavistic senses of nationhood that far transcend those loyalties applying to states in America, may continue to make unity difficult. Germany had certainly for decades been compliant in the unity project, not least because of its consciousness of its guilt for the events of 1933–45. However, restiveness in 2010 about Germany's supposed obligation to bail out economically weaker members of the EU who had fallen victim to their own economic delinquency stemmed from a growing belief that Germans, 65 years on, had apologised enough and made sufficient amends for their grandfathers' evil. Old ideas of nation die hard.

One principal means of achieving unity in Europe has since 1999 been through the attempt at a single currency. As was seen in the financial crisis after 2008, and not just in Germany, such a union strains the notion of supranationalism. When

Greece in particular was the beneficiary of a rescue package in 2010, German taxpayers asked why the fruits of their labours should be used to subsidise those not prepared to work so hard or take such risks. The answer was that it was in the interests of the European ideal. The German sense of national identity, consciously suppressed since 1945, is now sufficiently resurgent to find this problematical.

Robert Kagan argued in 2003 that the West was divided in its attitudes to the exercise of power for the future: 'One of the things that most clearly divides Europeans and Americans today is a philosophical, even metaphysical disagreement over where exactly mankind stands on the continuum between the laws of the jungle and the laws of reason.'[4] His argument is that Europe has chosen to pursue a Kantian 'perpetual peace' while America 'remains mired in history, exercising power in an anarchic Hobbesian world where international laws and rules are unreliable, and where true security and the defence and promotion of a liberal order still depend on the possession of military might'.[5] He contended that Europe, which now seeks to settle differences by the application of reason, has the luxury of doing so only because America is standing to one side waiting to settle things by the application of force. It is what Kagan calls the 'double standard' of America's advocating restraint by others while being always prepared itself to exercise force.

Kagan wrote those words before the full humiliation of the Bush regime in Iraq, and its further difficulties in Afghanistan. His original thesis was underpinned by a sense of certainty that America would prevail (even though the lesson of Vietnam should have made him cautious on that front), and would continue to allow Europe the luxury of elegant displays of rationality. History subsequently showed that American prevalence was not inevitable; that even an American administration, under George W. Bush's successor, could start to see the damage done to their nation's reputation in the world by the perceptions of the philosophy Kagan was expounding; and that an element of reasoning may, after all, have to be brought into play by a nation for which, hitherto, force had appeared to be enough.

Within a few years of Kagan's having written these opinions, his economic assumptions about the growing might of America began to look wrong and outdated; his understatement of the threat by China not so much in the military sense, but as an economic power, in relation to America looks ill-judged; and America, the once inevitably powerful, seems to be withdrawing within itself, thanks to a combination of falling reputation and growing economic troubles undermining its self-confidence, and a national debate about the nature of the American identity and values. The difficulty that America found itself in during the winter of 2011, when its former ally Hosni Mubarak was toppled by a popular uprising, demonstrated the decline of America's ability to change the weather in international relations. Egyptians proclaimed that this was their revolution, and not America's; and the concept of American intervention, toxified after the Iraq expedition, made it so.

Plainly, it is impossible accurately to predict the future course of history. The speed with which China, India and Brazil have grown as economies, and the potential they have to command markets around the world and to enrich themselves accordingly, have taken America very much by surprise; but then recent history has been full of surprises. The lingering shock of the end of the Soviet empire to those who benefited from it helps explain how difficult it has been for Russia to adjust to no longer having its neighbours as its supplicants. And the shock felt in America by the attacks of September 2001 was not least because the country's own intelligence services had not prepared the people for the eventuality of such a murderous assault, and the notion of the invulnerable home had never been challenged.

The split between the two wings of the West about how to exercise their power reflects the shift in the motivation for conflict. Having been used, for the whole of the 20th century, to fighting wars rooted in ideological differences, the West is now having to cope with an ill-defined religious insurgency with a strong ideological aspect. For America, the means it used to deal with threats during the Cold War – a nuclear arsenal and heavily funded conventional forces – remain. As for Europe, it has decided it would rather spend money on welfare than on arms; indeed in some of the constituent nations that had been decided before their own economic troubles forced retrenchment on all fronts. This was the so-called 'peace dividend' trumpeted by Western leaders immediately after the end of the Cold War.

Long before the rise of al-Qaeda, and long before the end of the Cold War, Europe had however been happy to shelter under the umbrella of a friendly superpower against a the threat of an unfriendly one. However, just as the nature of exertion of power appears to have changed one more time, from the martial to the diplomatic or economic, there is – as with Hitler, and Stalin's reversion to medievalism in the 20th century – evidence that a new reversion has taken place: the desire by militant Islam to impose its ideological-religious will by force of arms. Fukuyama asked: 'Is history directional, and is there reason to think that there will be a universal evolution in the direction of liberal democracy?'[6] If it was thought the answer was 'yes', there has been a diversion, or even a reverse, thanks to the surge of radical Islam. In the immediate aftermath of the regime changes in Tunisia and Egypt in 2011 it was clear that a transition to what the West calls 'democracy' could not be taken for granted: partly because of the survival of political vested interests, partly because of an opportunity presenting itself to Islamists who reject democracy on the Western model. Nor is an extreme religious ideology the only cause of a breach with the Fukuyama doctrine. There is also a retreat from democracy in post-Soviet Russia, and with it a disdain for democratic values such as the rule of law, blind justice, freedom from corruption and the resolution of differences by diplomatic means.

In his own extended rumination on the future, Huntington argued that the world order had been remade after the Cold War. Nations were no longer what mattered, but civilisations; and conflicts in future would largely occur between them. He drew a map of the main civilisations: Western, Latin American, African, Islamic, Sinic, Hindu, Orthodox, Buddhist and Japanese.[7] These divisions raise further questions: not least, as has been discussed, how coherent is the West? The Kagan thesis about the coherence of one of Huntington's civilisations, which is compelling, has it that the community of view between Europe and America may not last. Even within Europe there are divisions, based on different political cultures (such as dirigisme against liberal economics) and histories, and alignments continue to change.

The Orthodox civilisation includes some former Soviet republics whose relations with Russia are toxic and look likely to remain so. Two of the most powerful and rising civilisations, the Hindu and the Sinic, are for the most part nations – India and China. But Huntington's point is well made, not least because of the strong identification of common interests between nations in the Muslim world, sub-Saharan Africa, the English-speaking world (which through Britain has a bridge into Europe) and Latin American nations: though how far the last of those civilisations will remain coherent if Brazil surges far ahead of its neighbours is an interesting point. Finally, though not least, there are, as has been noted, similar tensions in post-banking-crisis Europe, because of the economic predominance of Germany.

Huntington's main point, as has been seen, is that power is shifting from its traditional home in Europe, and its recent home in America, to parts of the planet that used to be called 'third world': China, India, Brazil and, possibly, Russia, depending on its political stability, its conduct of international relations, and the value in the global marketplace of its natural resources. What marks Russia out from the other three powers is its determination to bring 20th-century methods into the 21st-century context to get its way. India has a long-standing issue with Kashmir, but otherwise it, China and Brazil see the acquisition of power now as something to be accomplished purely by economic success rather than by force and conquest. The idea that they wish to advance – even in its own way China – is capitalism.

Russia, as it showed in Georgia in 2008, is still willing to aggress against its neighbours if the opportunity arises. It has been destabilising in various ways its former possessions in the Baltic States, including by cyber-attack, and has raised aggressive protests against Poland when it was proposed to site an American missile shield on Polish soil. Whereas it seeks to acquire influence by intimidation, an emerging power such as China acquires it by investment: notably in regions such as sub-Saharan Africa.

In the 21st century power consists in some new, but also in some surprisingly traditional, forms. Who has the money and the arsenals it buys still matters profoundly; but who has the natural resources to survive and prosper becomes an ever more important consideration. Polities with both – and scarce resources will command high prices, thereby creating wealth and the ability to arm for those who have them – will inevitably take the commanding heights. Nor is energy the sole commodity that will confer power: water, biofuels, cultivable land and food will all become increasingly significant as populations grow and the means to keep them alive dwindles. Nations that offer expert services at competitive prices, such as Switzerland, or manufacture high-quality innovative goods, such as Japan, will always exercise considerable economic power. But in terms of the commodities that are likely to be important in the 21st century they will be customers rather than suppliers, and in a seller's market, with the constraints on their growth that that must entail.

The late 20th century saw various attempts by smaller polities to challenge or get on equal terms with superpowers by pooling power: as well as the European Union there was, in a different way, the Organisation of African Unity, which has sought to create a common voice for Africa without aspiring to any form of economic union; and the Association of South-East Asian Nations. There is an attempt under way to replace the Organisation of American States, which has long been regarded as a tool of United States policy, with a new Latin American power bloc whose 32 members met for the first time in February 2010 and excluded America and Canada.[8] Tensions within such actual or notional federations between established vested interests make them unstable and divisible. The real threat to established powers is either presented by the economic growth of rivals or by a ruthless decision to use force.

Just as the pursuit of power remains an eternal phenomenon, so too is it a constant truth that from economic power flow other forms of might. With seven admitted nuclear powers on earth (and for all one knows twice that number actually) the threat of mutually assured destruction still exists, and still holds back major powers from pursuing armed solutions to quarrels; this is the greatest change from even just a century ago.

With certain exceptions, such as the dispute over Kashmir or the insurgency in Chechnya, territorial ambitions no longer drive the pursuit of power. Even America's attempt at imperialism through the control of territory in Iraq was temporary, as it had had to be in Vietnam. The religious/ideological fervour of militant Islam seeks power for a renewed Caliphate; but China is conquering Africa by stealth, by massive economic investment and ownership of resources, not by imposing its rule or appointing governors-general. It is also making huge investments in European businesses. The martial and financial weakness of many sub-Saharan African countries makes such a stealthy imperialism possible in the way it is not in resource-rich but still economically fragile Russia. With oil and gas being finite resources, and often to be found in unstable polities, the pursuit of power to acquire the natural resources that sustain economies and living standards will in time become paramount; and many smaller and more vulnerable polities will find themselves marginalised or under serious economic threat. The fashionable, post-modern view is that in an age of democracies, power is widely dispersed through societies, weakening states and once-powerful institutions and the individuals who embody them. That can only be true so long as democracy pertains, and so long as post-democratic means are not deemed essential to maintain ways of life, living standards, and ultimately order.

It used to be a habit of leading powers that they became aggressive simply to protect their pre-eminence, for reasons already described in the thematic chapters of this essay. The pervasiveness of American influence around the globe after 1945, and especially after the dissolution of the Soviet bloc in the early 1990s, caused it to be disliked around the world for what was perceived to be neo-imperialism. The attacks on America in September 2001 may be interpreted as a feature of the backlash against this; its leadership of wars in Iraq and Afghanistan was certainly taken as further evidence of that trait. As soon as Russia felt rich enough to aggress against Georgia in 2008 it did so, partly to reassure its citizenry that the old swaggering image of the Cold War era had not entirely been given up. The world waits to see whether China will now put its economic might to martial use, in a useful exhibition of its potential muscle.

America remains, for the moment, the world's leading power as defined by the strength of its economy. Its crisis of confidence as it enters the second decade of this century is unlikely to be easily rectified. It is deeply divided politically. It is united by a fear, largely unspoken, of being overtaken by China, a country that thanks to its populousness is already more than America's equal militarily. China seems to have no martial intentions against its rivals, not least because it well understands how wars deplete economies; the power China seeks now is the power money can buy (notably acquiring assets around the globe), and the supply of money will be compromised if it chooses to engage in a conventional war. It uses other means of destabilising its rivals in order to steal economic advantage, such as cyberwar.[9] Russia has tried to use this weapon against its perceived enemies too, notably in the Baltic states.

Economic power is shifting from the West, because of the decadent principles upon which so many of its economies are run. There has been an addiction to debt; a commitment to excessive welfarism; over-regulation, especially of working practices; cartelisation; and the result of all this is a high cost base that reduces competitiveness. There are exceptions, such as Germany, which has combined fiscal rectitude with a manufacturing economy specialising in high-value, high-performance goods whose reputation defies a high exchange rate. But attempts to rein in spending and to remove the state from people's lives are not inevitably welcomed, as has been shown by the failure in France of President Sarkozy to implement, in the face of violent protests and strikes, the reform agenda he promised when elected in 2007. Only the imminence of bankruptcy seems to have the required salutary effect, as both Ireland and Greece demonstrated in 2010, the latter with great reluctance.

For the moment, Huntington's analysis holds

largely true. For all the rivalries within, say, the European Union, there is much evidence that European nations will come together if faced with a considerable threat from a rival civilisation. France, for example, was deeply opposed to the Iraq war in 2003. It has, however, been a consistent supporter of the attempt to root out nurseries of terrorism in Afghanistan, and its leaders have for the last decade voiced powerful opposition to the prospect of Iranian nuclear developments. There is solidarity in sub-Saharan Africa on behalf of nations criticised by the West – such as Zimbabwe has been – however justified that criticism might have been. The survival of Robert Mugabe, after three decades of systematic human rights abuse and the impoverishment of his mineral-rich nation, is not least down to the unwavering support of Jacob Zuma, the present President of South Africa, and his predecessor, Thabo Mbeki. Even if other African leaders do not share Mugabe's paranoia towards the white man, they do seem to regard it as culturally appropriate, in the terms of their civilisation, to give him moral support. There are many similar examples in the Islamic world of a failure to condemn, or even of support for, extremist activity in other Muslim countries.

America is a power whose vulnerability is revealed with increasingly frequency not just because of economic difficulties, but because of the attention paid to it by terrorists. Perhaps the next tectonic shift in history will come if America, sensing its own depletion even more keenly than at present, determines to withdraw from the world and look in again upon itself, as it did in the 1920s and 1930s. A problem with multi-trillion-dollar debt may in time limit what America feels it can practically achieve outside its own borders. On the southern of those borders it has the potential of a failed state in Mexico, whose troubles caused by a narco-war there are already spilling over into the United States. But in an age when the mass media purvey image more effectively than they purvey fact or reality, the most substantial pressure on America is the sense of its own unpopularity in the world. Sensitivity by Americans to accusations of cultural and physical imperialism is now acute, and could prove a driving force in reducing the nation's engagement with the world. This may be augmented by a chronic economic problem in America, burdened as it is by debt of incomprehensible size, and the need to retrench and reduce its role in the world while an economic reconstruction takes place.

In the last century or so the course of world history has been altered by assertions of all of the four main motivations behind the pursuit of power that have been outlined in this essay. Considerations of territory, the desire for wealth, the fervours of religion and of ideology have all provoked conflict and change. If history has not ended, its course has speeded up. No longer does one theme dominate whole centuries or epochs; the widespread existence of autonomous and ambitious polities means that conflicts are more likely, more frequent, and liable to be caused by any of the main influences. The course of history will continue to move in the unstable and unpredictable way it has since 1914. The competition is still on, even if the development of civilisation dictates that some of the natural competitors must find more subtle methods of playing. The triumph of liberal democracy remains an unfinished victory.

The Western, democratic civilisation is on the defensive. The ideas of Hobbes, Machiavelli and Nietzsche all compete to undermine it. Idealism is threatened by the realities of human nature. The worst form of complacency in the West would be to continue to believe that our own values are so superior that they cannot in the long term be challenged by those of others – especially if the machines of repression prove to function successfully in the factories of prosperity. The first step in the defence of democracy must be to recognise that the desire of others to assert their power, for their reasons, is as pervasive as our own. If we use our liberties to allow our own value system to be undermined, then we shall lose them.

– Notes –

1 Introduction

1 'The End of History' in
The National Interest 16
(Summer 1989).

2 Huntington, *passim*. (Exact
details of all works cited in
footnotes are to be found
in the Bibliography.)

3 Carlyle II, p.13.

4 Aristotle, p.120.

5 Gibbon, Vol. I, p.77.

6 Carlyle V, p.162.

7 Butterfield, p.9.

8 Ibid., p.11.

9 Fulford, pp.298–304.

10 Hinsley, p.290.

11 Lebow, p.20.

12 Said, p.204.

13 See, for example, Russell,
pp.291–315.

14 Aristotle, p.115.

15 Plato (trans. Waterfield),
Chapter 9.

2 Land

1 Darwin, p.165.

2 Grote, IV, pp.385ff.

3 Creasey, p.2.

4 Kershaw I, pp.247–50.

5 Finlay, p162.

6 Ibid, pp.37–8.

7 A point argued controver-
sially in Fitzjames Stephen,
pp.112–15.

8 Mommsen, III, p.60.

9 Thierry, I, p.143ff.

10 Poole, p.378.

11 Green, I, pp.265–6.

12 Wilson, pp.751ff.

13 Hinsley, p.177.

14 See, for example, Trevelyan,
Vol. I, p.123, on the dangers
to British trade and security
if France were allowed to
take the Spanish throne.

15 Zamoyski, pp.377ff.

16 Hinsley, p.252.

17 Lebow, pp.61–72.

18 Tooze, pp.145–6.

19 Mulligan, pp.62ff.

20 Joll, quoted in Mulligan,
p.14.

21 Finlay, p.11.

22 Ibid., p23.

23 Ibid., p.24.

24 Powicke, Chap.13, describes how this had advanced by the late 13th century.

25 Finlay, p.177.

26 Ibid., p.207.

27 Ibid., p.263.

28 Huntington, p.253.

29 Lebow, pp.236ff.

30 Harvey II, pp.9–15.

31 Hitler, p.587.

3 God

1 Exodus 17:16, Numbers 31:3.

2 Isaiah 2:4.

3 Prescott, p.115; Thomas, pp.60, 347.

4 Riley-Smith, p.5.

5 St Augustine, p.518.

6 Lewis, pp.70ff.

7 Gibbon, VI, pp.15–17.

8 Tyerman, p.352.

9 Ibid., p.68.

10 Ibid., p.67.

11 Ibid., pp.305–6.

12 Finlay, p.342.

13 Ibid., p.352.

14 Ibid., p.353.

15 Ibid., p.355.

16 Carr, p.310.

17 Gibbon, Vol. II, Chapters XV and XVI *passim*.

18 Gibbon, Vol. VII, p.308.

19 Wilson, *passim*.

20 Buckle, Vol. I, p.266.

21 Lee, p.203.

22 Ibid.

23 See, for example, Weber, pp.147–8.

24 Schumpeter, p.11.

25 See, notably, Chadwick, pp.107–39.

26 Hobbes, part 3.

27 Wright, p.133.

28 Ibid, p.79.

29 *Washington Post*, 24 June 2008.

30 Huntington, p.252.

31 See, for example, 'The Discomfort of Strangers', David Goodhart, *Guardian*, 24 February 2004.

4 Wealth

1 See for example Blanning, pp.93–141.

2 Mommsen, II, 5.

3 Grote, XI, pp.467–97.

4 Finlay, p.29.

5 Finlay, p.110.

6 Wilson, p.429.
7 Arnold, p.78.
8 Russell, p.118.
9 Stern, pp.176–225.
10 Simms, pp.579–635.
11 Fukuyama, p.73.

12 Mulligan, p.7.
13 See, for example, Schumpeter, p.165.
14 Finlay, p.410.
15 Ibid., p.412.
16 Shirer, p.256.

5 Minds

1 Marx and Engels, p.34.
2 Ibid., p.52.
3 Ibid., p.58.
4 Hitler, p.20.
5 Ibid., p.3.
6 Ibid., p.10.
7 Ibid., p.14.
8 Ibid., p.53.
9 Blanning, pp.624–33.
10 Thucydides, p.49.
11 Lebow, p.180.
12 Marx and Engels, p.64.
13 Hobbes, Chapter 13.
14 See his essay 'Shooting Niagara: and After?' in Carlyle VI.

15 Made *passim* in *Reflections on the Revolution in France*.
16 Harvey, p.73.
17 Ehrman, Vol II, p.258.
18 Hinsley, p.221.
19 Trevelyan, p.155.
20 Nietzsche I, pp.171–2.
21 Nietzsche II, *passim*, but notably in part IV.
22 Weber, pp.287–91.
23 Service, p.59.
24 Ibid., p.79.
25 Ibid., p.132.
26 Conquest, pp.171–221; Sebag Montefiore, pp.242–54.

6 Future

1 Fukuyama, p.xv.
2 See particularly Fukuyama, pp.xi–xxiii.
3 Hayek, *passim*.
4 Kagan, p.91
5 Ibid., p.3.
6 Fukuyama, p.71.
7 Huntington, pp.26–7.

8 See 'Latin America's path to independence', Mark Weisbrot, *Guardian*, 26 February 2010.
9 See, for example, 'The On-line Threat', Seymour M. Hersh, *The New Yorker*, 1 November 2010.

– Bibliography –

The Anglo-Saxon Chronicles, trans. James Ingram (Dent, 1922)

Aristotle: *Politics*, trans. B. Jowett (OUP, 1916)

Arnold: *The Vikings: Culture and Conquest*, by Martin Arnold (Continuum, 2006)

Blanning: *The Pursuit of Glory: Europe 1648–1815*, by Tim Blanning (Viking, 2007)

Bracher: *Turning Points in Modern Times*, by Karl Dietrich Bracher (Harvard, 1995)

Bryce: *The Holy Roman Empire*, by James Bryce (Macmillan, 1901)

Buckle: *A History of Civilisation in England*, by H. T. Buckle (OUP, 3 vols., 1903)

Bullock I: *Hitler: A Study in Tyranny*, by Alan Bullock (BCA, 1973)

Bullock II: *Hitler and Stalin: Parallel Lives*, by Alan Bullock (HarperCollins, 1991)

Burleigh I, *Earthly Powers*, by Michael Burleigh (HarperCollins, 2005)

Burleigh II: *Sacred Causes*, by Michael Burleigh (HarperCollins, 2006)

Burke: *Reflections on the Revolution in France*, by Edmund Burke (vol. IV of the Works, OUP, 1907)

Butterfield: *The Whig Interpretation of History*, by Herbert Butterfield (Bell, 1968)

Caesar: *The Gallic Wars*, by Julius Caesar, trans. H. J. Edwards (Heinemann, 1966)

Carlyle I: *The French Revolution*, by Thomas Carlyle (vols. II–IV of the Centenary Edition, Chapman and Hall, 1898)

Carlyle II: *Heroes, Hero-Worship and the Heroic in History* by

Thomas Carlyle (vol. V of the Centenary Edition, Chapman and Hall, 1901)

Carlyle III: *Past and Present*, by Thomas Carlyle (vol. X of the Centenary Edition, Chapman and Hall, 1899)

Carlyle IV: *The History of Frederick the Great* (vols. XII–XIX of the Centenary Edition, Chapman and Hall, 1897)

Carlyle V: *Critical and Miscellaneous Essays*, vol IV (vol. XXIX of the Centenary Edition, Chapman and Hall, 1899)

Carlyle VI: *Critical and Miscellaneous Essays*, vol V (vol. XXX of the Centenary Edition, Chapman and Hall, 1899)

Carr: *Blood and Faith*, by Matthew Carr (Hurst, 2009)

Chadwick: *The Secularisation of the European Mind in the 19th Century*, by Owen Chadwick (CUP, 1975)

Clark: *Iron Kingdom: The Rise and Downfall of Prussia 1600–1947*, by Christopher Clark (Allen Lane, 2006)

Conquest: *Stalin: Breaker of Nations*, by Robert Conquest (Weidenfeld and Nicolson, 1991)

Cowling: *Religion and Public Doctrine in Modern England*, by Maurice Cowling (CUP, 3 vols., 1980–2001)

Darwin: *After Tamerlane*, by John Darwin (Allen Lane, 2007)

Dehio, Ludwig: *The Precarious Balance: The Politics of Power in Europe, 1494–1945* (Chatto and Windus, 1963)

Ehrman: *The Younger Pitt*, by John Ehrman (3 vols., Constable, 1969–96)

Fest: *Hitler*, by Joachim Fest (Weidenfeld and Nicolson, 1974)

Finlay: *Greece under the Romans*, by George Finlay (Dent, 1906)

Fitzjames Stephen: *Liberty, Equality, Fraternity*, by James Fitzjames Stephen (CUP, 1967)

Froude I: *Henry VIII*, by James Anthony Froude (3 vols., Dent, 1909)

Froude II: *Edward VI*, by James Anthony Froude (Dent, 1910)

Froude III: *The Reign of Mary Tudor*, by James Anthony Froude (Dent, 1910)

Froude IV: *Elizabeth*, by James Anthony Froude (5 vols., Dent, 1912)

Fukuyama, *The End of History and the Last Man*, by Francis
  Fukuyama (Hamish Hamilton, 1992)

Fulford: *Votes for Women*, by Roger Fulford (Faber, 1957)

Gibbon: *The Decline and Fall of the Roman Empire*, by Edward
  Gibbon, ed. J. B. Bury (7 vols., Methuen, 1896–1900)

Green: *A Short History of the English People*, by J. R. Green
  (2 vols., Dent, 1915)

Grote: *A History of Greece*, by George Grote (12 vols., Dent,
  1907)

Hallam: *The Constitutional History of England*, by Henry
  Hallam (3 vols., Dent, 1926)

Harvey I: *Liberators: Latin America's Struggle for Independence*,
  by Robert Harvey (John Murray, 2000)

Harvey II: *The War of Wars*, by Robert Harvey (Constable, 2007)

Haslam: *Russia's Cold War*, by Jonathan Haslam (Yale, 2011)

Hayek: *The Road to Serfdom*, by Friedrich von Hayek
  (Routledge, 1944)

Herodotus: *The History of Herodotus*, trans. J. E. Powell (2 vols.,
  OUP, 1949)

Hinsley: *Power and the Pursuit of Peace*, by F. H. Hinsley (CUP,
  1963)

Hitler: *Mein Kampf*, by Adolf Hitler, trans. Ralph Manheim
  (Pimlico, 1992)

Hobbes: *Leviathan*, by Thomas Hobbes (Oxford World's
  Classics, 2008)

Huntington: *The Clash of Civilisations and the Remaking
  of World Order*, by Samuel P. Huntington (Simon and
  Schuster, 1996)

Irving I: *The Warpath*, by David Irving (Michael Joseph, 1978)

Irving II: *Hitler's War*, by David Irving (Hodder and Stoughton,
  1977)

Kagan: *Paradise and Power: America and Europe in the New
  World Order*, by Robert Kagan (Atlantic, 2004)

Kershaw I: *Hitler: Hubris*, by Ian Kershaw (Allen Lane, 1998)

Kershaw II: *Hitler: Nemesis*, by Ian Kershaw (Allen Lane, 2000)

Lebow: *A Cultural Theory of International Relations*, by Richard Ned Lebow (CUP, 2008)

Lecky I: *A History of European Morals from Augustus to Charlemagne*, by W. E. H. Lecky (2 vols., Longmans, 1905)

Lecky II: *The Rise and Influence of Rationalism in Europe*, by W. E. H. Lecky (2 vols., Longmans, 1904)

Lecky III: *The History of England in the 18th Century*, by W. E. H. Lecky (7 vols., Longmans, 1904)

Lecky IV: *Democracy and Liberty*, by W. E. H. Lecky (Longmans, 1896)

Lee: *Aspects of European History 1494–1789*, by Stephen J. Lee (Routledge, 2nd edition, 1984)

Lewis: *God's Crucible: Islam and the Making of Europe, 570–1215*, by David Levering Lewis (W. W. Norton, 2008)

Macaulay: *The History of England from the Accession of James II*, by Thomas Babington Macaulay (3 vols., Dent, 1906)

Machiavelli: *The Prince*, by Niccolo Machiavelli, trans. George Bull (Penguin, 2003)

Marx/Engels: *The Communist Manifesto*, by Karl Marx and Frederick Engels, with an introduction by Eric Hobsbawm (Verso, 1998)

Marx: *Capital*, by Karl Marx, trans. Eden and Cedar Paul (Everyman, 1930)

Mommsen: *The History of Rome*, by Theodor Mommsen, trans. W. P. Dickson (4 vols., Dent, 1911)

Motley: *The Rise of the Dutch Republic*, by J. L. Motley (3 vols., Dent, 1906)

Mulligan: *The Origins of the First World War*, by William Mulligan (CUP, 2010)

Nietzsche I: *The Will to Power*, by Friedrich Nietzsche, edited by Walter Kaufmann (Vintage, 1968)

Nietzsche II: *Beyond Good and Evil*, by Friedrich Nietzsche (Penguin, 1990)

Nietzsche III: *Thus Spoke Zarathustra*, by Friedrich Nietzsche (Penguin, 1969)

Plato: *The Republic*, by Plato, trans. R. Waterfield (OUP, 1993)

Poole: *From Domesday Book to Magna Carta*, by A. L. Poole (OUP, 2nd edition, 1955)

Powicke: *The Thirteenth Century*, by Maurice Powicke (OUP, 2nd edition, 1962)

Prescott: *The History of the Conquest of Peru,* by William H. Prescott (Dent, 1908)

Preston: *Franco*, by Paul Preston (HarperCollins, 1993)

Riley-Smith: *The Crusades, a Short History*, by Jonathan Riley-Smith (Yale, 1987)

Roberts: *Masters and Commanders*, by Andrew Roberts (Allen Lane, 2009)

Russell: *Prince Henry 'the Navigator': A Life*, by Peter Russell (Yale, 2000)

Said: *Orientalism*, by Edward W. Said (Pantheon, 1978)

St Augustine: *The City of God*, by St Augustine, trans. Marcus Dods (Digireads.com, 2009)

Schumpeter: *Capitalism, Socialism and Democracy*, by Joseph A. Schumpeter (Harper Perennial, 2008)

Sebag-Montefiore: *Stalin: The Court of the Red Tsar*, by Simon Sebag-Montefiore (Weidenfeld and Nicolson, 2003)

Seeley I: *The Expansion of England*, by J. R. Seeley (Macmillan, 1883)

Seeley II: *The Growth of British Policy*, by J. R. Seeley (2 vols., CUP, 2nd edition 1897)

Service: *Trotsky, A Biography*, by Robert Service (Macmillan, 2009)

Shirer: *The Rise and Fall of the Third Reich*, by William L. Shirer (Secker and Warburg, 1960)

Sidgwick: *The Development of European Polity*, by Henry Sidgwick (Macmillan, 1920)

Simms: *Three Victories and a Defeat: The Rise and Fall of the First British Empire, 1714–1783*, by Brendan Simms (Allen Lane, 2007)

Sismondi: *The History of the Italian Republics*, by J. C. L. de
    Sismondi (Dent, 1907)

Stern: *Gold and Iron: Bismarck, Bleichroder and the Building of
    the German Empire*, by Fritz Stern (Penguin, 1987)

Strachan: *The First World War*: Vol. I, *Call to Arms*: (OUP, 2001)

Stubbs: *The Constitutional History of England in its Origin and
    Development*, by William Stubbs (3 vols., OUP, 1891)

Taylor I: *The Origins of the Second World War*, by A. J. P. Taylor
    (Hamish Hamilton, 1961)

Taylor II: *The Struggle for Mastery in Europe*, by A. J. P. Taylor
    (OUP, 1954)

Thierry: *The Norman Conquest of England*, by A. Thierry
    (2 vols., Dent, 1906)

Thomas: *The Conquest of Mexico*, by Hugh Thomas
    (Hutchinson, 1993)

Thucydides: *The Peloponnesian Wars*, trans. Rex Warner
    (Penguin, 1972)

Tooze: *The Wages of Destruction: The Making and Breaking of
    the Nazi Economy*, by Adam Tooze (Pengin, 2006)

Trevelyan: *England under Queen Anne* (3 vols.), by G. M.
    Trevelyan (Longmans, 1930–4)

Tyerman: *God's War: A New History of the Crusades*, by
    Christopher Tyerman (Allen Lane, 2006)

Weber: *Political Writings*, by Max Weber, edited by Peter
    Lassman and Ronald Spiers (CUP, 1994)

Wickham: *The Inheritance of Rome: A History of Europe*, by
    Chris Wickham (Allen Lane, 2009)

Wilson: *Europe's Tragedy: A History of the Thirty Years War*, by
    Peter Wilson (Allen Lane, 2009)

Woodruff: *The Struggle for World Power 1500–1980*, by William
    Woodruff (Macmillan, 1981)

Zamoyski: *1812: Napoleon's Fatal March on Moscow*, by Adam
    Zamoyski (HarperCollins, 2004)

– Acknowledgements –

This book arose out of a series of conversations and exchanges several years ago with Stuart Proffitt, who shaped my thinking on this question to a profound degree, though all the responsibility for what appears here is mine and mine alone. I am grateful to him and hope he feels the trouble he took in discussing these ideas was worthwhile, even if not profitable. I am indebted to Dr Lucasta Miller for agreeing to take this project on, and for her intelligent and highly perceptive guidance during the course of it. Michael Burleigh, to whom this work is dedicated, gave me some invaluable guidance early on and exerted a moral and intellectual influence whose full extent he will be too modest to appreciate. I wrote the book during a sabbatical year, for which I must thank the Chief Executive of the Telegraph Media Group, Murdoch MacLennan. It was written at Corpus Christi College, Cambridge, during a year as Fellow Commoner, and I must sincerely thank the Master, Stuart Laing, and the Fellows for their hospitality and many other kindnesses. I greatly benefited particularly from conversations with Professor Jonathan Haslam, Sarah Cain and Dr Pernille Røge, and notably from a seminar I led with Dr Røge's history students. Professor Brendan Simms and Professor Christopher Clark also gave me important and helpful ideas, for which I thank them. My agent, Georgina Capel, was especially supportive on the long journey of such a short book. Finally, nothing would have been possible without the constant support and understanding of my wife, and I thank her above all others.

nh